A Curious History
of Food and Drink

A Curious History
of Food and Drink

Ian Crofton

Quercus

First published in Great Britain in 2013 by
Quercus Editions Ltd
55 Baker Street
Seventh Floor, South Block
London
W1U 8EW

p1 Mary Evans Picture Library / Alamy; p8 Mary Evans Picture Library /
Alamy; p12 Mary Evans /Grenville Collins Postcard Collection; p25 The
Granger Collection / Topfoto; p68 Topfoto; p77 The Granger Collection /
Topfoto; p89 The Granger Collection / Topfoto; p101 Fortean / Topfoto; p127
The Granger Collection / Topfoto; p104 The Art Archive / Amoret Tanner
Collection; p137 The Art Archive / DeA Picture Library / M. Seemuller; p145
The Art Archive; p157 Picturepoint / Topfoto; p191 Picturepoint / Topfoto;
p188 RONALD GRANT ARCHIVE/ArenaPAL / Topfoto; p259 Popperfoto/
Getty Images; p210 Shutterstock; p269 Print Collector / HIP /TopFoto; p283
Shutterstock; p290 The Art Archive / NGS Image Collection; p328 RIA Novosti
/ TopFoto; p337 Keystone/Getty Images; p330 Sean Gallup/Getty Images

A CIP catalogue record for this book is available
from the British Library

ISBN 978 1 78206 940 9

10 9 8 7 6 5 4 3 2 1

Text designed and typeset by Ellipsis Digital Ltd

Printed and bound in Great Britain by Clays Ltd, St Ives plc

Menu

Introduction

Quite when humans first became cooks will probably never be known for certain, although circumstantial evidence indicates that it may have been almost 2 million years ago. Even before that time, our ancestors must have experimented with a wide range of raw wild foods – not just meat, fish and insects, but also fruits, nuts, grains and fungi. No doubt there were instances of heroic self-sacrifice (or sheer greed and stupidity) when certain individuals found they could not resist a particularly alluring bunch of shiny red berries, or that patch of pretty yellow toadstools. Their uncomfortable ends no doubt provided a dire – and evolutionarily useful – warning to others.

By and large, humans – especially in the West – have narrowed the range of foods that they willingly consume, as compared to what they *could* consume. Insects and their grubs have pretty much disappeared from the menu, although in these pages you will find such delicious snacks as succulent honey ants, crispy cockchafer larvae, and cicadas dipped in chocolate. The Romans delighted in such dishes as the teats of sows and cows, rabbit foetuses, and

– if they could get hold of them – the brains of pheasants and flamingos. Today, however, our willingness to eat all parts of a slaughtered animal – surely an ethical imperative if one is going to eat meat at all – is very much on the decline. For example, cow's udder, which so pleased Samuel Pepys, is now rarely encountered, while the consumption of testicles (in the English-speaking world at least) is largely restricted to the more boisterous regions of the American West.

Similarly, our ancestors would consider cooking and eating any wild animal that came their way – from elephant, giraffe and hippo, to squirrel, badger and even fox (apparently not worth the effort). The nutritional value of such foods cannot be doubted, but the same cannot be said for sawdust, or grass mowings, or mud from the bottom of Lake Victoria – which have all had their enthusiastic, if eccentric, advocates.

A Curious History of Food and Drink does not just deal with unusual foodstuffs, however. There are descriptions of bizarre and extravagant banquets, both real and fictional, from the Feast of Trimalchio in the *Satyricon* (in which one of the highlights was 'live fish swimming in wine') to the dinner of the Company of the Saucepan in Renaissance Florence, which featured a temple made of sausages, Parmesan, gelatine, sugar and marzipan. Then, in contrast, there was the 'The Banquet of the Underfed', described by a 16th-century Bolognese poet, which included such dishes as fly-head pie, jellied bat's foot and stewed spleen of spring frog. Securing enough to eat was also on the minds of the 15,000-strong crowd who gathered in Denby Dale in Yorkshire in 1846 to grab their share of the giant pie baked to celebrate the repeal of the Corn Laws, which had kept so many hungry for so long.

This book also contains numerous accounts of the origins of various dishes, from Chicken Marengo, Spanish Omelette and Nesselrode Pudding, to Sandwiches, Sachertorte and Tournedos Rossini. It turns out in many cases that the popularly peddled tales of these culinary births are not necessarily as historically sound as we previously thought – but why spoil a good story . . . In addition, throughout the book the reader will find various historical recipes, from the Roman sauce made from fermented anchovy guts to the mock fish conjured out of ground rice in the darker days of the Second World War. Then there is the Renaissance peacock served in its feathers and with flames coming out of its mouth, a medieval English recipe for lamprey cooked in its own blood, and a 12th-century Indian king's favourite dish – roast rat. None of these recipes have been tested by the present author, and are included for historical interest only. It goes without saying that any readers attempting to follow any of these recipes do so entirely at their own risk . . .

A Curious History of Food and Drink also pays attention to the more human dimensions of culinary history. Thus we hear from Pope Gregory the Great on the five forms of gluttony and Gautama Buddha on the five worldly benefits of porridge; from Benjamin Franklin on the avoidance of asparagus-scented urine and William Cobbet on the detrimental consequences of drinking tea – plus D.H. Lawrence on Spanish wine, Kingsley Amis on Spanish food, P.J. O'Rourke on French cheese, and Miss Piggy (an underappreciated authority) on the best way of avoiding snails. Then there is the Greek philosopher Democritus surviving on the smell of freshly baked bread, Cleopatra vying with Mark Antony to see who could put on the most lavish feast, Moctezuma taking chocolate to boost his amatory appetites, and the French chef who was so ashamed when the fish did not arrive in time for a royal banquet that he ran himself through with his own sword. In more recent times one might mention Fatty Arbuckle's talents with custard pies, Marilyn Monroe's stint as Artichoke Queen of Castroville, the deadly aversions of Presidents Nixon and Bush snr for certain green vegetables, and astronaut John Glen getting into trouble over a corned-beef sandwich – not to mention Monsieur Mangetout (the man who ate an entire light aircraft), the musical and gastronomic talents of the Viennese Vegetable Orchestra, and Lady Gaga's campaign against Baby Gaga, the ice cream made from human breast milk.

The great French gastronome Jean Anthelme Brillat-Savarin famously declared that 'The discovery of a new dish confers more happiness on humanity than the discovery of a new star.' This book is for all those food-lovers who are ever eager to hear about new, strange and wonderful dishes (although they may draw the line at human flesh, which crops up in these pages every now and again). *A Curious History of Food and Drink* is definitely *not* for those to whom, in Brillat-Savarin's words, 'nature has denied an aptitude for the enjoyments of taste'. Such people, Brillat-Savarin continues, 'are long-faced, long-nosed and long-eyed; whatever their stature, they have something lanky about them. They have dark, lanky hair, and are never in good condition. It was one of them who invented trousers.' Those who sit back after a good meal and happily loosen their belts may feel inclined to agree. It is to them that this book is dedicated.

Ian Crofton
London, October 2013

PREHISTORY

1.9 million years ago

The First Cooks Research by Harvard scientists published in 2011 suggests that it was one of our early ancestors, *Homo erectus*, who first learnt to cook, some 1.9 million years ago. This is because of the relatively small size of the molars of *Homo erectus* as compared to other apes, which indicates that our ancestors may only have spent 7 per cent of their day feeding, while the chimpanzee, for example, spends over a third of its day eating. Only by cooking food, the Harvard scientists propose, could *Homo erectus* have managed with such small molars, avoiding the tedious business of endless chewing. Cooking also enabled these early ancestors to extract more calories from their food and to broaden their diet – a crucial step in the evolution of humanity.

circa 100,000 BC

The Marks on the Bones In the 1990s archaeologists examining a Neanderthal site in a cave at Moula-Guercy in southern France uncovered human bones marked by numerous grooves. Some believe the grooves may have been made by the teeth of wild animals, while others contend that they are the result of ritual de-fleshing. However, as similar marks are found on the bones of roe deer that had been butchered by Neanderthal tools, the suggestion is that this particular group of Neanderthals, at least, were cannibals.

In 2009, archaeologists excavating near the village of Herxheim in Germany's Rhineland-Palatinate found a large collection of much more recent bones – those of modern humans from around 5000 BC. The bones, which cover a period of several decades, showed clear signs of butchery. Ritual de-fleshing is again a possibility – but so, too, is cannibalism.

circa 6000 BC

Hippo Soup The earliest soup that archaeologists have found evidence of dates from around 6000 BC, and contained the bones of a hippopotamus. A more recent recipe for hippo soup can be found in *The Albert N'yanza, Great Basin of the Nile* (Vol. I, 1867), the account by the English explorer Sir Samuel Baker of his discovery of Lake Albert in Africa in 1864:

A new dish! There is no longer mock-turtle soup – REAL turtle is MOCK HIPPOPOTAMUS.

I tried boiling the fat, flesh and skin together, the

3

result being that the skin assumes the appearance of the
green fat of the turtle, but is far superior.

A piece of the head thus boiled, and then soused in
vinegar, with chopped onions, cayenne pepper and
salt, throws brawn completely in the shade.

My men having revelled in a cauldron of hippopotamus soup, I serve out grog at sunset . . .

According to old Africa hands, the fat of the hippo
is so sweet it can − with relish − be eaten raw.

           ＿   ＿   ＿

circa 2000 BC

The Earliest Noodles In 2005 archaeologists uncovered
the world's oldest noodles in Lajia, China, at the site of
an ancient earthquake. The 4000-year-old noodles, which
had been buried with an earthenware bowl, quickly oxi-
dized and turned to dust on exposure to the air, but from
the remnants scientists determined they had been made
from millet.

circa 1400 BC

A Brief History of Xocoatl The earliest evidence of the
cultivation of cacao trees − from which we obtain choco-

late – comes from a site in Honduras and dates from around 1400 BC. The word chocolate itself probably derives from the Nahuatl word *xocoatl*, meaning 'bitter water'. Nahuatl was the language spoken by the Aztecs, who were great drinkers of chocolate – Moctezuma, the last Aztec emperor, would fortify himself by drinking a bowlful before visiting his courtesans.

The first European to taste *xocoatl* was the Spanish conquistador Hernán Cortés, who in 1519 was presented with a bowl while he was a guest of the Aztecs (he later showed his gratitude by turning on his hosts and destroying them). Later in the century, José de Acosta, a Spanish Jesuit missionary in the New World, described chocolate as 'loathsome to such as are not acquainted with it, having a scum or froth that is very unpleasant to taste'. He continues:

> Yet it is a drink very much esteemed among the Indians, wherewith they feast noble men who pass through their country. The Spaniards, both men and women that are accustomed to the country are very greedy of this chocolate. They say they make diverse sorts of it, some hot, some cold, and some temperate, and put therein much of that 'chilli'; yea, they make paste thereof, the which they say is good for the stomach and against the catarrh.

The impact of chilli in one's chocolate, as favoured by the natives of Central America in the 16th century, was described by Edward R. Emerson in *Beverages, Past and Present* (1908):

> One small sip of this chocolate is generally enough to make a man think that he has awakened in another world, and all doubt about which one it is is removed at once. The outside world has very little interest for him at this time. It is the inside one that calls for immediate attention.

The new drink caught on in Spain, where the chilli was dispensed with and replaced by sugar, vanilla and cinnamon. In the 17th century the fashion spread to France – where some believed it could have unlooked for consequences, as recounted in a letter by Madame de Sévigné:

> The Marquise de Coëtlogon took too much chocolate, being pregnant last year, that she was brought to bed of a little boy who was as black as the devil. It died.

London's first chocolate house was opened in 1657, the French proprietor asserting that the drink 'cures and preserves the body of many diseases'. Many more chocolate houses followed, although they were briefly closed down in 1675, as Charles II feared they were hornet's nests of sedition.

In 1689 in Jamaica, Sir Hans Sloane, the noted physician and collector, first added milk to the drink, a combination subsequently prescribed by apothecaries for various ailments. Jean Anthelme Brillat-Savarin celebrates chocolate as a universal panacea in his *Physiologie du goût* ('Physiology of Taste'; 1825):

Let, then, every man who has drunk too deeply from the cup of pleasure, every man who has devoted to work a considerable part of the time due to sleep, every man of wit who feels that he has temporarily become stupid, every man who find the air damp, the weather unendurable, or time hanging heavy on his hands, every man tormented with some fixed idea which deprives him of the liberty of thinking – let all such people, we say, prescribe to themselves a good pint of chocolate mixed with amber in the proportion of from sixty to seventy grains to the pound, and they will see wonders.

So far, so liquid. It was not until 1847 that the British Quaker company of Joseph Fry and Co found a way of making solid chocolate, and created the first chocolate bar.

THE ANCIENT WORLD

circa 650 BC

On the Antiquity of Liquorice The earliest reference to liquorice, found on some stone tablets from Baghdad, dates from around 650 BC. The Assyrians used liquorice as a treatment for sore feet, and as a diuretic. The word itself derives from Greek *glykyrrhiza*, meaning 'sweet root'. It was the Romans who brought liquorice from the Mediterranean to Britain, where it is particularly associated with the town of Pontefract (or Pomfret) in Yorkshire. The story goes that in the 16th century a Pontefract schoolmaster, visiting the east coast of England, found some liquorice sticks washed up on the shore from an Armada wreck. He used these sticks to beat his pupils, who would bite on one of the sticks while being thrashed, and so discovered a delicious new flavour. The town subsequently became famous for its flat, round liquorice sweets, known as Pomfret cakes.

circa 600 BC

The Soup of Venus The city of Marseille was founded by a Greek people called the Phoceans. It is these people that the modern-day inhabitants of the city credit with creating their most famous dish – the fish soup called bouillabaisse. The word bouillabaisse is a combination of two

Occitan words, *bolhir*, 'to boil', and *abaissar*, 'to lower the heat' – referring to the method of bringing the stock to the boil, adding another ingredient, bringing it back to the boil and then reducing the heat to a simmer. In Roman mythology, it was a soup of this kind that Venus, goddess of love, fed to her husband Vulcan, while she enjoyed an assignation with her lover Mars, god of war.

circa 535 BC

The Five Benefits of Porridge At the outset of his quest for enlightenment, Gautama Buddha followed the path of self-mortification, sustaining himself on no more than a nut or a leaf per day until he became so weakened and starved that a village girl called Sujata thought that he was a spirit. However, she managed to revive him with a bowl of rice porridge and milk, and thereafter Gautama expounded upon the five benefits of porridge: it improves the digestion, quenches the thirst, suppresses hunger, deals with constipation and reduces wind. It was after this incident that Gautama realized that enlightenment would only come via the Middle Way, the path between self-indulgence and extreme asceticism.

circa 440 BC

The Fat-tailed Sheep of Arabia In his *Histories*, the Greek author Herodotus (known both as the 'father of history' and the 'father of lies') describes two remarkable kinds of sheep found in Arabia, 'the like of which are nowhere else to be seen':

> One kind has long tails no less than four and a half feet [1.35 metres] long which, if they were allowed to trail on the ground, would be bruised and develop sores. As it is, the shepherds have enough skill in carpentry to make little carts for their sheep's tails. The carts are placed under the tails, each sheep having one to himself, and the tails are then tied down upon them. The other kind has a broad tail which is at times 18 inches [45 centimetres] across.

Although the modern fat-tailed sheep cannot boast such magnificent appendages, they continue to be the dominant form across North Africa and the Middle East. The fat in the fat tails differs from normal body fat in that it melts much more easily, and it has long been a valued cooking oil in the cuisine of the region. In addition, the meat of fat-tailed sheep tends to be leaner than that of their thin-tailed cousins (breeds of which dominate in Europe and elsewhere), as the fat of the former is concentrated in the tail rather than the legs and trunk.

401 BC

Toxic Honey In the *Anabasis*, the account by the Greek writer and soldier Xenophon of his retreat across Asia Minor from his disastrous Persian campaign, we read of the consequences of eating honey derived from the mauve-flowered *Rhododendron ponticum*:

> The effect upon the soldiers who tasted the combs was, that they all went for the nonce quite off their heads, and suffered from vomiting and diarrhoea, with a total inability to stand steady on their legs. A small dose produced a condition not unlike violent

12

drunkenness, a large one an attack very like a fit of madness, and some dropped down, apparently at death's door. So they lay, hundreds of them, as if there had been a great defeat, a prey to the cruellest despondency. But the next day, none had died; and almost at the same hour of the day at which they had eaten they recovered their senses, and on the third or fourth day got on their legs again like convalescents after a severe course of medical treatment.

The poisons responsible were grayanotoxins, found in rhododendrons and other ericaceous plants. Symptoms of grayanotoxin poisoning include salivation, perspiration, dizziness, loss of coordination, severe muscular weakness and a slowing of the heart rate. Only very occasionally does grayanotoxin poisoning prove fatal; otherwise recovery is quick. The army of the Roman general Pompey, campaigning in Asia Minor in 69 BC, also suffered from the effects of eating toxic honey.

circa 400 BC

A Dish Worse than Death? The standard fare of the Spartans – who despised any form of luxury – was the infamous *melas ẓomos* or 'black broth', a bitter gruel of pork stock, vinegar and salt. The vinegar may have acted as an emulsifier to stop the pig's blood clotting during cooking. One appalled visitor from Sybaris (the Greek city in southern Italy that gave us the word 'sybaritic') reported:

> It is natural enough for the Spartans to be the bravest of men; for any man in his senses would rather die ten thousand times over than live as miserably as this.

> Quoted in Athenaeus, *The Deipnosophistai*
> (*circa* AD 200)

circa 370 BC

A Drastic Diet In old age, the Greek philosopher Democritus is said to have cut out something from his meals every day until death eventually came to him. According to his biographer Hermippus of Smyrna (*fl.* 3rd century BC), when the philosopher was nearing his end, his sister was concerned that his death would prevent her from worshipping at the three-day festival of Thesmophoria. To allay her anxieties, Democritus kept himself alive till the festival was over by breathing in the smell of freshly baked loaves. He then passed away in peace.

circa 350 BC

On the Deliciousness of Nymphs In his *History of Animals*, Aristotle commends the eating of cicadas, especially the nymphs, as the adults have a harder exoskeleton. But if one must eat an adult, he advises, go for an egg-laden female.

circa 300 BC

On the Origins of Cinnamon Although the cinnamon tree is native to Sri Lanka, the ancients believed the spice originated in Arabia. Theophrastus, Aristotle's successor at the Lyceum in Athens, reported as follows:

> They say it grows in valleys where there are snakes with a deadly bite, so they protect their hands and feet when they go down to collect it. When they have brought it out they divide it into three portions and draw lots for them with the Sun, and whichever portion the Sun wins they leave behind. As soon as they leave it, they say, they see it burst into flames. This is of course fantasy.

257 BC

Make Me Vegetarian, But Not Yet Ashoka the Great, also known as Piyadasi, ruler of a great empire that stretched even beyond the bounds of present-day India, issued a number of edicts embodying his Buddhist beliefs, and had them carved on stone pillars across his realm. Among his pronouncements was this promise of a gradual introduction of vegetarianism:

> Formerly, in the kitchen of Beloved-of-the-Gods, King Piyadasi, hundreds of thousands of animals were killed every day to make curry. But now with the writing of this Dhamma edict only three creatures – two peacocks and a deer – are killed, and the deer not always. And in time, not even these three creatures will be killed.

circa 250 BC

A Love of Pungency The Roman comedy writer Plautus decried the habit of some cooks of over-flavouring their dishes with sharp herbs and heavy spices, describing their seasonings as like 'screech owls eating the entrails out of living guests'. The Romans certainly liked strong flavours, as attested by their love of *garum*, the ubiquitous salty sauce made from fermented fish, which they ate with virtually everything. The recipes of Apicius, probably dating from the 1st century AD, show how pervasive the Roman love of strong flavours was – for example, his recipe for flamingo includes vinegar, dill, coriander, pepper, caraway, asafoetida root, mint, rue and dates. The same recipe works equally well, says Apicius, for parrot. As for *garum* (also known as *liquamen* or *muria*), Apicius has a recipe for an expensive version using the livers of red mullet, and a peculiarly pungent version using fish blood, gills and guts, together with salt, vinegar, wine and herbs. This concoction was left out to ferment in the sun for three months, then strained and bottled. *Garum* was manufactured on a large scale in many Roman towns, and sometimes the smell became so overpowering that the authorities would temporarily suspend production.

Fermented Fish Guts

The 10th-century Byzantine compilation known as the *Geoponica* gives a recipe for *garum*, that favourite sauce of the ancient Romans:

> Add a quantity of salt in the ratio of one to eight to the entrails of any small fish, such as mullets, sprats or anchovies.

Allow the mixture to ferment in the sun for
several months.

Draw off the liquid and strain it.

Use as a condiment on just about any dish
you care to name.

In his *Epistles*, the Roman dramatist Seneca complained that *garum* 'burns up the stomach with its salted putrefaction', while the poet Martial declares, in his *Epigrams*, that a man who can maintain his passion for a girl who has just gobbled up six helpings of *garum* deserves every sort of commendation.

— — —

circa 200 BC

The Ayurvedic Diet Some of the earliest texts of Ayurvedic medicine were compiled in India around 200 BC. In Ayurveda, eating the right food is regarded as essential to health, and to this end, foods are divided into hot and cold, with six flavours: pungent, acidic, salty, sweet, astringent and bitter. Hot foods, including meat and pepper, are salty, acidic or pungent, and can (according to the theory) cause sweating, inflammation, thirst, fatigue and fast digestion. Cold foods, such as fruit and milk, are bitter, astringent or sweet, and induce calm and contentment. During hot weather, cold foods such as milky gruels help the body to conserve energy. In cooler weather, it is possible to eat heavier foods, such as fatty meat, wine and honey, as the body can spare the energy to digest them. Where one lives must also be taken into account: in dank, marshy regions people should eat hot, heavy foods such as lizard meat, while plain-dwellers should eat light dishes such as black antelope. Much Indian cookery today seeks to blend hot and cold foods, and various subtle combinations of the six flavours.

Holy Cows At this early stage in India, the eating of beef – subsequently completely taboo among Hindus – was tolerated, and indeed the *Mahabharata* mentions Brahmans (members of the priestly caste) sitting down to hearty meals of beef. However, the medical texts warn that, as beef is 'heavy, hot, unctuous and sweet', it is hard to digest and should only be eaten with caution, by those who lead physically active lives. Beef broth, however, was regarded as an excellent medicine, especially for those with any sort of wasting disease. The consumption of beef continued at least into the 1st century AD.

The transformation of the cow into a sacred animal probably resulted from its increasing importance as a draught animal and as a source of milk. The Italian traveller Niccolao Manucci, who spent much time at the

Mughal court in the 17th century, wrote in his *Storia do Mogor* that 'these people hold it an abomination to eat of the cow', and described how the Hindus, in order to purge their sins, would consume a mixture of the cow's holy products: milk, butter, dung and urine.

181 BC

Sumptuary Laws In an effort to counter what was regarded as creeping decadence, the Roman Senate enacted the *Lex Orchia*, which, as well as specifying what kinds of clothes persons of different ranks could wear, restricted the number of diners one could invite to a banquet. This was followed in 161 BC by the *Lex Fannia*, which limited the number of dishes one could consume at a meal to three (five if it was a special celebration). Exotic foods such as shellfish and 'strange birds from another world' were banned, while a later law, the *Lex Aemilia*, forbade that favourite Roman delicacy, stuffed dormice.

Sumptuary laws – although almost impossible to enforce – continued to be enacted through the Middle Ages and beyond. An English law of 1336 banned people from consuming more than two courses at any one meal, although three were allowed on feast days – and it was specifically stated that soup counted as a full course, not just as a sauce. Another English law, passed in 1517, set limits on the number of courses dependent on one's rank: cardinals were permitted nine courses; dukes, archbishops, marquesses, earls and bishops were allowed seven; lesser lords, mayors of the City of London, knights of the garter and abbots were allowed six. Those whose income was less than £100 but more than £40 could look forward to a mere three courses.

Similar distinctions are found in other cultures. When Sir Thomas Roe was in India between 1615 and 1619 as King James I's ambassador to the Mughal court, his chaplain, Edward Terry, noted that at a banquet he, being of junior rank, was served ten fewer dishes than Sir Thomas. It turned out that a common-or-garden reverend had to be content with a mere fifty bowls.

circa 100 BC

Payment in Salt Part of the pay awarded to Roman soldiers was called the *salarium*, as it was intended for the purchase of salt (Latin *sal*) – valuable both for flavouring and for preserving food. The word later denoted their entire pay – hence our word 'salary', and also the expression 'not worth his salt'. The word 'salad' also ultimately derives from the same root, salt being a key ingredient in the green salads prepared by the Romans.

63 BC

On the Importance of Maintaining Standards The Roman general Lucius Licinius Lucullus returned triumphant from the Third Mithradatic War in Asia Minor, accompanied by so much booty that he established himself as one of the richest men in Rome. He was renowned for his magnificent building projects, his patronage of the arts and sciences, and his hosting of spectacularly lavish feasts. Plutarch tells us that one evening Lucullus was dining alone – a rare occurrence – and was dismayed to find that his table did not boast its accustomed glory. He registered his dissatisfaction with a servant, who apologetically explained that as the master was dining alone it had been assumed that he would not require the usual sumptuous fare. Lucullus was not to be mollified. 'Do you not realize,' he roared, 'that tonight Lucullus dines with Lucullus?'

43 BC

A Noble Roman Called Chickpea The Roman orator and political writer Marcus Tullius Cicero died on 7 December. His surname was said by Plutarch to have been awarded to one of his ancestors on account of a blemish on his nose shaped like a chickpea – *cicer* in Latin. It is more likely, however, that his ancestors did well out of the chickpea business. Other noble Roman families also had leguminous surnames: Lentulus means 'lentil', Piso 'pea' and Fabius (as in Quintus Fabius Cunctator, the general whose delaying tactics wore down Hannibal's army in Italy, and whose name was adopted by the Fabian Society) means 'bean'.

circa 40 BC

Bathing in Ass's Milk Cleopatra, queen of Egypt, was said to bathe daily in ass's milk in order to maintain the youthfulness and beauty of her skin. Some 700 asses were apparently required to provide her with sufficient milk for her daily bath. In his *Natural History* (1st century AD), Pliny the Elder recounts the cosmetic advantages of ass's milk:

It is generally believed that asses' milk effaces wrinkles in the face, renders the skin more delicate, and preserves its whiteness: and it is a well-known fact that some women are in the habit of washing their face with it seven times daily, strictly observing that number. Poppaea, the wife of the Emperor Nero, was the first to practise this; indeed, she had sitting-baths prepared solely with asses' milk, for which purpose whole troops of she-asses used to attend her on her journeys.

Pliny recommends ass's milk for a number of medical complaints, from fever and ulcers to asthma and constipation, and as a specific against certain poisons, including white lead. This was probably why in the Elizabethan era some wealthy women used ass's milk to clean off their face paint – which largely consisted of white lead.

circa 35 BC

Extravagance In his *Parallel Lives*, Plutarch gives the following account of Mark Antony's dining arrangements when the great Roman general was in Egypt with his lover Cleopatra:

> At any rate, Philotas, the physician of Amphissa, used to tell my grandfather, Lamprias, that he was in Alexandria at the time, studying his profession, and that having got well acquainted with one of the royal cooks, he was easily persuaded by him (young man that he was) to take a view of the extravagant preparations for a royal supper. Accordingly, he was introduced into the kitchen, and when he saw all the other provisions in great abundance, and eight wild boars a-roasting, he expressed his amazement at what must be the number of guests. But the cook burst out laughing and said: 'The guests are not many,

only about twelve; but everything that is set before them must be at perfection, and this an instant of time reduces. For it might happen that Antony would ask for supper immediately, and after a little while, perhaps, would postpone it and call for a cup of wine, or engage in conversation with some one. Wherefore,' he said, 'not one, but many suppers are arranged; for the precise time is hard to hit.'

Antony and Cleopatra used to wager with each other as to who could put on the most expensive banquet. After one such feast, hosted by Cleopatra, Antony observed that it seemed no more lavish than the one he had put on the previous evening. At this, Cleopatra took a great pearl from her ear, ground it up and sprinkled it in her wine, which she drained to the last dregs. The wager was won.

Anchovy Casserole without the Anchovies

This is the translation of the Latin *Patina de apua sine apua*, a recipe from *De re coquinaria*, the celebrated collection of recipes by Apicius, a wealthy Roman merchant and gourmet who lived in the 1st century AD. Here is his recipe:

Finely chop enough roasted or boiled anchovies to fill a casserole dish of whatever size you like.

Take some pepper and a little bit of rue; add a sufficient amount of broth to cover and a little bit of olive oil and mix together in the casserole with the fish.

Then beat raw eggs and mix all the ingredients together in the casserole.

Arrange sea nettles on top, but do not mix them with the eggs.

Cover the casserole, being careful that the nettles do not mix with the eggs, and when the liquid has

> evaporated, sprinkle with ground pepper and serve.
> No one at the table will know what he is eating.

This last cryptic comment – and the name of the recipe itself – suggests that the dish is of such subtlety (note that it involves fresh rather than salted anchovies) that the actual ingredients are transmuted out of all recognition.

AD 43

An Easement of the Law Under the Emperor Claudius, the Roman Senate passed a law permitting the passing of wind at banquets. Claudius had been worried that holding gas in could damage one's health.

AD 55

Food Taster Fails to Forestall Fatality In Rome, Britannicus, the 13-year-old son of the late Emperor Claudius and rival to Nero as heir to the emperor's purple, became the victim of a cunning plan. Being offered a drink at a banquet, he had his food taster check it first. The food taster sipped, and did not expire, so passed the cup to Britannicus. The latter found the drink too hot, so a servant called Locusta (probably also responsible for serving the Emperor Claudius with fatally toxic mushrooms) cooled it down with water. Locusta had previously laced the water with poison, and Britannicus fell to the floor foaming at the mouth, and in an instant was dead. Nero claimed the boy had suffered a severe epileptic fit.

— ~ —

The Feast of Trimalchio

In his *Satyricon*, the Roman courtier and writer Gaius Petronius Arbiter (d. AD 66) mocked the pretensions of the nouveau riche. In the section entitled 'The Feast of Trimalchio', the guests of the freed slave Trimalchio are plied with more and more outrageous and impossible dishes. Paring things down, one might extrapolate the following simplified menu from Petronius' lavish descriptions:

White and black olives

Dormice seasoned with honey and poppies

Sausages brought in piping hot on a silver gridiron, and
under that large damsons, with the kernels
of pomegranates

THE ANCIENT WORLD

Mock peahen's eggs of pastry surrounding peppered
egg yolk stuffed with a delicate
fat wheatear

The hinder paps of a sow

Live fish swimming in wine

A hare with the fins of fish stuck in its sides, so making it
resemble a flying horse

A boar of the first magnitude, surrounded by marzipan
piglets and stuffed with live blackbirds, which fly out
when the boar's side is pierced

A whole hog, which, when its stomach is sliced
opened, lets fall a heap of sausages, as if it were being
disembowelled

A young boiled heifer with a helmet on
her head, sliced up by a man playing the mad Ajax,
who serves the joints to the guests on the tip of
his sword

A service of cheesecakes and tarts, stuck
round with all manner of apples and grapes, which,
upon the least touch, throw out a
delicious liquid perfume

AD 69

The Shield of Minerva According to the Roman historian Suetonius, the Emperor Vitellius dispatched emissaries to distant parts of the empire to find pike livers, brains of pheasants and flamingos, and the milt of lampreys – all crucial ingredients for a dish called 'The Shield of Minerva'. One of the emperor's regular dining companions, after he had missed some days' banqueting due to illness, thanked heaven that he had been unwell, 'Otherwise,' he said, 'I would be dead.' Vitellius himself only remained emperor for eight months; in December he was put to death on the orders of his successor Vespasian.

AD 79

Beetroot, Boron and Bunga-Bunga The Roman town of Pompeii was destroyed by an eruption of Vesuvius. Among the frescoes in the brothels found in the ruins are some that show people drinking what appears to be red wine, but which scholars now believe may be beetroot juice, which was valued as an aphrodisiac in the classical world. Seeds and other traces of beetroot have also been found at the site by archaeologists. The fact that the vegetable is high in the mineral boron, which may encourage the production of sex hormones, lends some credence to the old belief.

Fig-filled Pigs In his *Natural History*, published shortly before his death in the eruption of Vesuvius, Pliny the Elder describes how his near-contemporary, the gourmet Apicius, adapted the well-established method of over-feeding geese to enlarge their livers (a practice known in Egypt as long ago as 2300 BC):

> Apicius made a discovery, that we might employ the same artificial method of increasing the size of the liver of a sow, as with that of the goose. It consists in cramming them with dried figs and when they are fat enough, they are drenched with wine mixed with honey, and immediately killed.

So closely did the fig become associated with liver that *foie*, the modern French word for 'liver', actually derives from the Latin *ficatum*, 'fig'.

circa AD 90

A Morbid Feast The Emperor Domitian held a banquet at which the guests were ushered into a gloomy room, where, to their alarm, they noticed that their places were indicated by tombstones. Naked dark-skinned boys served burnt meat on black plates, while the emperor talked of nothing but sudden death and murder. The guests must have thought they had fatally incurred the emperor's displeasure. But when they returned to their homes they found that Domitian had sent, not the expected executioner, but a rich gift for each guest.

A similarly gloomy dinner was hosted in Paris on 1 February 1783 by a 24-year-old called Alexandre-Balthazar-Laurent Grimod de la Reynière – who was later generally acknowledged as the first professional food critic. Grimod had sent out invitations in the form of a death notice, and when his guests arrived, they found a coffin in the centre of the table and one candle for every day of the year. The event shocked respectable Paris society, and became known as the *souper scandaleux* ('scandalous supper'). As a consequence, Grimod's embarrassed family disinherited him and sent him off for a while to live in a monastery.

Many years later, in 1812, Grimod, having alienated many people in Paris and having failed to disguise his antipathy towards Napoleon, sent out a notice announcing his own death, together with the date and time at which his funeral cortège would leave his house in the Champs-Elysées. When his few close friends turned up at his house at the appointed hour, they found a bier in the hall, surrounded by candles. They were then ushered in silence into an inner room, where to their astonishment they found a table set out for a feast, with a grinning Grimod welcoming them at the head of the table – delighted that he had exactly matched the number of place settings to the number of his true friends.

circa AD 100

Getting the Hang of Decadence The Roman poet Martial noted in his *Epigrams* that among the dishes served at the banquets of the wealthy was 'teat of a sow's udder' – Martial complained that one guest swept more than his fair share into his napkin to take home with him. Such was the aura of greed, it was not unknown for Roman gourmands to train themselves to tolerate the hottest of dishes so that they could finish them before the other guests, and thus have first stab at the tastier dishes to follow. Around the same time as Martial was writing, the satirist Juvenal, as well as mocking the desire of his fellow citizens for nothing other than 'bread and circuses', ridiculed the fact that a rich man called Crispinus had spent 6000 sesterces on a 6-pound (2.7-kilogram) mullet.

Other delicacies favoured by those Romans who could afford them included rabbit foetuses, the vulvas of sows and cows, snails fattened on milk and wheat until they could no longer fit in their shells, and thrushes reared on millet and figs chewed up for them by slaves. Those wanting to make a bigger splash served goatfish, which were placed on the table alive so that guests could appreciate the vivid red their scales turned as they suffered a slow, suffocating death. Another status symbol was Trojan pig, a supposedly humorous play on the story of the Trojan horse, in which a whole pig was roasted, stuffed with sausages and served standing on its feet. Its belly was then cut open, and out would tumble the sausages, looking just like the animal's entrails.

THE MIDDLE AGES

circa AD 600

Defining Gluttony Pope Gregory I, known as Gregory the Great, defined five aspects of gluttony, one of the seven deadly sins, citing biblical passages in justification:

1. Eating before mealtimes: Thy father [Saul] straitly charged the people with an oath, saying, Cursed be the man that eateth any food this day. And the people were faint. Then said Jonathan, My father hath troubled the land: see, I pray you, how mine have been enlightened, because I tasted a little honey.

1 Samuel 14:28–29

2. Seeking out delicacies and finer foods to gratify the 'vile sense of taste': And the mixt multitude that was among them fell a lusting: and the children of Israel also wept again, and said, Who shall give us flesh to eat? We remember the fish, which we did eat in Egypt freely; the cucumbers, and the melons, and the leeks, and the onions, and the garlick: But now our soul is dried away: there is nothing at all, beside this manna, before our eyes. Numbers 11:4–6

3. Seeking after sauces and seasoning: The basis of this seems to be that Hophni and Phinehas, the sons

of the High Priest Eli, kept all the best bits of meat from the sacrifices for themselves, and were slain for their sins.   1 Samuel 4:11

4. Eating too much: Behold, this was the iniquity of thy sister Sodom, pride, fullness of bread, and abundance of idleness was in her and in her daughters, neither did she strengthen the hand of the poor and needy.   Ezekiel 16:49

5. Being over-eager to eat, even if it is plain fare, and one does not eat excessively: The biblical exemplar is Esau, who famously sells his birthright to his brother Jacob for 'bread and pottage of lentiles'.   Genesis 25:29–34

732

A Bull Against Horse Pope Gregory III issued a papal bull banning the consumption of horse meat, condemning it as 'an unclean and execrable act'. His aim was to support St Boniface's mission to evangelize Germany, where the pagan tribes had apparently eaten horse as part of ceremonies associated with the worship of Odin. The Norse inhabitants of Iceland also had a penchant for horse meat, and for this reason resisted conversion to Christianity until

999, when they gained a special dispensation from the Church.

circa 800

On the Protective Quality of Garlic Anglo-Saxon herbals advised a mixture of garlic, bitter herbs, leeks, fennel, butter and mutton fat as a sure-fire way of protecting oneself against malevolent elves.

An Irish Fighting Feast The Irish saga *Scéla Mucce Meic Dathó* ('The Tale of Mac Dathó's Pig') describes how at a feast the warriors fall out over who is entitled to the 'champion's portion', i.e. the best cut of meat:

> Blows fell upon ears until the heap on the floor reached the centre of the house and the streams of gore reached the entrances. The hosts broke through the doors, then, and a good drinking bout broke out in the courtyard, with everyone striking his neighbour.

circa 850

Kaldi and the Coffee Beans According to legend, an Arabian goatherd called Kaldi noticed that his flock became much livelier after they fed on the bright red berries of a certain bush. He tried the berries himself, and the exhilaration he subsequently experienced led him to take the berries to a Muslim holy man. The latter disapproved, however, and threw the berries into the fire – unleashing a wonderful aroma. Anxious to capture this wonder, Kaldi raked the roasted beans from the fire, pounded them into a powder, dissolved them in hot water – and so made the first cup of coffee.

The story of Kaldi did not appear in written form until 1671, however, and the tale is almost certainly apocryphal: the wild coffee plant is native to Ethiopia, and may not have been introduced to Arabia until the 15th century. The word itself may derive from the Ethiopian kingdom called Kaffa, which emerged in the late 14th century. Arab lexicographers, however, suggest that the Arabic word *qahwah* (pronounced *kahveh* by the Turks) originally denoted some kind of wine, and ultimately derived from the verb *qahiya*, 'to have no appetite' – which is certainly one of the effects of a strong input of caffeine.

857

Polluted Rye The *Annales Xantenses*, compiled in Cologne, recorded that in this year 'a great plague of swollen blisters consumed the people by a loathsome rot, so that their limbs were loosened and fell off before death'. This is thought to be the first recorded reference to the gangrenous effects of ergotism, also known as St Anthony's fire or dancing mania, a condition contracted by eating rye bread (or other cereal products) contaminated with *Claviceps purpurea*. This fungus produces alkaloids that cause not only gangrene, but also convulsions and hallucinations – one of the alkaloids, ergotamine, has structural similarities with LSD. Outbreaks continued in Europe through to the later 19th century.

circa 880

Murderous Oxen Banned from Table A law enacted during the reign of Alfred the Great made it an offence to consume an ox that had gored a person to death. The beast was instead to be executed by stoning.

circa 900

A Riddle The Anglo-Saxons delighted in the following riddle:

I am a wonderful creature, bringing joy to women, and useful to those who dwell near me. I harm no citizen except only my destroyer. My site is lofty; I stand in a bed; beneath, somewhere, I am shaggy. Sometimes the very beautiful daughter of a peasant, a courageous woman, ventures to lay hold on me, assaults my red skin, despoils my head, clamps me in a fashion. She who thus confines me, this curly haired woman, soon feels my meeting with her – her eye becomes wet.

The answer is: an onion.

Help for Husbands Bald's *Leechbook* – an Anglo-Saxon herbal – recommends that men troubled by endless female chatter should consume a radish before retiring at night.

1104

The Dunmow Flitch Lady Juga Bayard established a tradition at Dunmow in Essex, by which any person who knelt down on two sharp stones at the church door and who could swear that for a year and a day he had not been involved in any domestic dispute or wished himself unmarried would be awarded a flitch (side) of bacon. The tradition appears to have persisted for some centuries, and is mentioned, for example, in 'The Wife of Bath's Prologue and Tale' in Chaucer's *Canterbury Tales*:

> The bacon was nat fet for hem, I trowe,
> That som men han in Essex at Dunmowe.

The tradition was revived in 1855, since when, in June of

every leap year, a flitch of bacon is awarded to any married couple judged by a jury of six local bachelors and six local maidens to have lived in complete content and harmony over the previous year and a day.

Roast Rat à la Manasollasa

King Somesvara III, who ruled the Western Chalukya empire in southern India between 1126 and 1138, was the author of the Sanskrit classic *Manasollasa* ('Refresher of the Mind'), a book largely devoted to princely pleasures, especially food. He describes a great range of dishes, from lentil dumplings in spicy yoghurt sauce and fatty pork with cardamoms to fried tortoise and roasted rat. Here is his recipe for the latter:

Select a strong black rat, found in the fields and
river banks.

Fry it in hot oil holding it by the tail till the
hair is removed.

After washing with hot water, cut open the stomach and
cook the inner parts with sour mango and salt.

Alternatively, skewer the rat and roast it over
red-hot coals.

When the rat is well cooked, sprinkle it with salt, cumin and lentil flour.

~ ~ ~

1135

A Surfeit of Lampreys King Henry I of England died on 1 December, at the age of 66 or 67, supposedly of a 'surfeit of lampreys' (although it was more likely food poisoning). Henry was in Normandy at the time, and one day, according to the contemporary chronicler Henry of Huntingdon, was so hungry after hunting that he ordered a dish of lampreys. The lamprey, a parasitic jawless fish of unprepossessing appearance, was long regarded as a delicacy. However, according to the doctrine of the humours, it was considered to be dangerously cold and wet (even more so than other fish), so had to be killed by being immersed in wine, and was then roasted with warming herbs and spices. Henry's own physician had warned him against them, but the king ignored his advice, and at once suffered 'a most destructive humour' accompanied by 'a sudden and severe convulsion'. He died shortly afterwards, and his corpse was sewn into a bull's hide before being returned to England, where he was buried at Reading Abbey.

Despite this warning tale, lampreys continued to be

prized in England up until the 19th century, and are still eaten in the Loire region of France, and (hot and smoked) in Finland. In 1633 the diarist Samuel Pepys celebrated the anniversary of the removal of a kidney stone – a painful operation from which he was lucky to survive – with a dish to which he was particularly partial: lamprey pie.

Sauce Pour Lamprey

The following recipe for lamprey comes from *A Noble Boke of Cokery*, a manuscript from the mid-15th century.

Take a quick [living] lamprey, and let him bleed at the navel, and let him bleed in an earthen pot;

And scald him with hay, and wash him clean, and put him [on a spit;] and set the vessel with the blood under the lamprey while he roasteth, and keep the liquor that droppeth out of him;

And then take onions, and myce [dice] them small, And put them in a vessel with wine or water, And let them parboil right well; And then take away the water, and put them in a fair vessel;

And then take powder of canell [cinnamon or cassia]

and wine, And draw them through a strainer,
and cast [them to] the onions, and set over the fire, and
let them boil;

And cast a little vinegar and parsley thereto, and a little
pepper; and then take the blood and the dropping of
the lamprey, and cast thereto [and] let boil together till it
be a little thick, and cast thereto powder ginger, vinegar,
salt, and a little saffron;

And when the lamprey is roasted enough, lay him in a
fair charger, and cast all the sauce upon him, and so
serve him forth.

circa 1150

An Unfortunate Side-effect The physicians at the
renowned medical school at Salerno in southern Italy realized that garlic was a two-edged sword in the fight against
disease. They encapsulated their views in the following
couplet:

Since garlic then hath powers to save from death,
Bear with it though it makes unsavoury breath.

Seven centuries later Mrs Beeton, in *The Book of Household
Management* (1861), dismissed garlic altogether: 'The smell

45

of this plant is generally considered offensive, and it is the most acrimonious in its taste of the whole of the alliaceous tribe.'

Peppercorn Rents During the civil war between Stephen and Matilda, rivals for the throne of England, coinage became so scarce that rents were paid in valuable spices, especially peppercorns, as these could not be debased – unlike silver. By the 19th century the price of pepper had fallen in relative terms and a peppercorn rent came to mean a notional rent. The phrase is still sometimes taken literally. For example, in Bermuda the Masonic Lodge of St George's No. 200 has every year since 1816 paid a single peppercorn to the island's governor, presented on a silver plate, for the rental of the Old State House, which is used as their lodge. Things are a little pricier in England: the Sevenoaks Vine Cricket Club in Kent has to pay two peppercorns every year to the town council for the use of their ground and pavilion.

1154

Pasta Arrives in Italy In the *Kitab nuzhat al-mushtaq* (often translated as 'A Diversion for the Man Longing to Travel to Far-Off Places'), the Arab geographer Muhammad al-Idrisi, who lived in Sicily at the court of King Roger II, made the first mention of pasta on Italian soil. It comes in his description of Trabia, a town east of Palermo:

> West of Termini there is a delightful settlement called Trabia. Its ever-flowing streams propel a number of mills. Here there are huge buildings in the countryside where they make vast quantities of *itriyya*, which is exported everywhere: to Calabria, to Muslim and Christian countries. Very many ship-loads are sent.

Itriyya is mentioned some two centuries earlier in an Arabic medical text written by a Jewish doctor in what is now Tunisia, and was the word for long thin strands of dried dough which were cooked by boiling. If the *itriyya* made in Sicily in al-Idrisi's time was so widely exported, it must (like modern dried pasta) have been made from durum wheat – 'hard' wheat – to enable it to keep well enough to travel. The word *itriyya* is not in fact Arabic, but rather an Arabic transliteration of a Greek word for some kind of dough-based food cooked by boiling – but whether this might have resembled pasta cannot at this distance be established with even the remotest degree of certainty.

Incidentally, the commonly told story that it was the medieval Venetian traveller Marco Polo who introduced pasta to Italy, in imitation of the noodles he had eaten in

China, is just that – a story. However, it was one that proved hard to kill. In 1929 the *Macaroni Journal*, the organ of the US National Macaroni Manufacturers Association, carried a short tall story called 'A Saga of Cathay', in which a sailor called Spaghetti, who accompanied Marco Polo on his voyage, visits a Chinese village:

> His attention was drawn to a native man and woman working over a crude mixing bowl. The woman appeared to be mixing a bowl of some kind, particles of which had overflowed the mixing bowl and extended to the ground. The warm, dry air, characteristic of the country, had in a short time hardened these slender strings of dough, and had made them extremely brittle.

Signor Spaghetti observes that these slender strings are delicious once boiled in salted water.

The *Macaroni Journal* may have been gently pulling its readers' legs, but in the lavish 1938 Samuel Goldwyn film *The Adventures of Marco Polo*, the hero, played by Gary Cooper, is entertained by an elderly Chinese philosopher called Chen Tsu, who – in all seriousness – offers him bowls of what he calls *spa get*. So impressed is Marco Polo that he takes some dried *spa get* back to Venice. A cuisine is born.

circa 1180

London's First Fast-food Outlet? In William FitzStephen's *Descriptio Nobilissimi Civitatis Londoniae* ('Description of the Most Noble City of London'), which forms the preface to his biography of his late martyred master Thomas Beckett, there is a description of a 'public cookshop' on the River Thames:

> On a daily basis there, depending on the season, can be found fried or boiled foods and dishes, fish large and small, meat – lower quality for the poor, finer cuts for the wealthy – game and fowl (large and small). If friends arrive unexpectedly at the home of some citizen and they, tired and hungry after their

journey, prefer not to wait until food may be got in and cooked, or 'till servants bring water for hands and bread', they can in the meantime pay a quick visit to the riverside, where anything they might desire is immediately available. No matter how great the number of soldiers or travellers coming in or going out of the city, at whatever hour of day or night, so that those arriving do not have to go without a meal for too long or those departing leave on empty stomachs, they can choose to detour there and take whatever refreshment each needs. Those with a fancy for delicacies can obtain for themselves the meat of goose, guinea-hen or woodcock – finding what they are after is no great chore, since all the delicacies are set out in front of them. This is an exemplar of a public cookshop that provides a service to a city and is an asset to city life. Hence, as we read in Plato's *Gorgias*, cookery is a flattery and imitation of medicine, the fourth of the arts of civic life.

circa 1188

When is a Bird a Fish? Giraldus Cambrensis (Gerald of Wales), in his *Topographia Hibernica*, gave the following account of the barnacle goose:

They are produced from fir timber tossed along the sea, and are at first like gum. Afterwards they hang down by their beaks as if they were a seaweed attached to the timber, and are surrounded by shells in order to grow more freely. Having thus in process of time been clothed with a strong coat of feathers, they either fall into the water or fly freely away into the air. They derived their food and growth from the sap of the wood or from the sea, by a secret and most wonderful process of alimentation. I have frequently seen, with my own eyes, more than a thousand of these small bodies of birds, hanging down on the seashore from one piece of timber, enclosed in their shells, and already formed. They do not breed and lay eggs like other birds, nor do they ever hatch any eggs, nor do they seem to build nests in any corner of the earth.

The common medieval belief that barnacle geese developed from the marine crustacean after which they are named meant, somewhat conveniently, that these birds counted as fish, and could therefore be eaten on meat-free fast days. (In much the same way, centuries ago in Venezuela, the Catholic Church issued a dispensation allowing the consumption of the capybara – the world's largest rodent – during Lent, on the grounds that as it spent most of its life in water it must be a fish.)

The mystery of the origin of barnacle geese was eventually dispelled when in 1597 sailors from William Barents' expedition found their nests on the remote islands of Novaya Zemlya, deep inside the Arctic Circle.

circa 1200

Belching at the Ceiling Around this time Daniel of Beccles wrote his *Book of the Civilized Man* (*Urbanus Magnus Danielis Becclesiensis* in Latin), which included a number of words of advice on table manners, such as:

> When eating at the table of the wealthy, refrain from garrulousness.
> Should you desire to belch, remember first to gaze up at the ceiling.
> If you need to clear your nose, do not show others what appears in your hand.
> Do not omit to thank your host.
> Abstain from mounting your horse in the hall.

And (a relief for those visiting the smallest room in the castle):

> It is unseemly to fall upon your enemy while he is voiding his bowels.

The author also believed that it was impolite for guests to pass water in the dining hall – but that it was perfectly permissible for the host to do so. Finally, if while dining at one's lord's table, the lord's wife expresses her desire for carnal knowledge, the best thing to do is to pretend to be ill.

Some Medieval Jests In the Middle Ages, the cooks in the great castles liked to play jokes on the guests. Live birds were indeed hidden in pies (like the 'four-and-twenty blackbirds' of the nursery rhyme), so that when the crust was cut open they would fly out. Then there were mock oranges: balls of saffron-coloured rice stuffed with minced meat and mozzarella that the Normans called *arancina* (from Arabic *arangio*, meaning 'bitter orange'). The Arabs themselves may have learnt the joke from the Persians. Another dish that was not quite what it seemed was the Cockatrice, the mythical beast that was half snake and half bird, which was recreated by sewing the front end of a chicken to the back end of a suckling pig, the whole thing then being covered in pastry and baked. Perhaps the most belly-splitting jape of all involved presenting one's guests with slabs of beef straight from the fire, sprinkled with tiny slivers of raw heart – which would writhe around on the hot meat just like maggots.

1274

Concentrating the Mind through the Stomach Pope Gregory X issued *Ubi periculum*, which laid out some rules for the conclave of cardinals summoned to elect a new pope. This was prompted by the previous election, in which the squabbling cardinals, meeting at Viterbo, had taken 33 months to come to a decision, and this only after the citizens of Viterbo, sick of playing host to the princes of the Church, removed the roof of their residence and supplied them with only bread and water. This had the desired effect, and Gregory was elected in 1271 as the compromise candidate. His own rules for the conclave laid down, among other things, that if the cardinals had not agreed who should be the new pope within three days, they would be allowed no more than two meals a day, each consisting of no more than one dish; and if after a further five days no decision had been made, then the cardinals were to be reduced to bread and water.

In 1353, the bull *Licet in constitutione* allowed for a supplement of salad, fruit, soup and a little sausage to be added to the two basic meals, and by the conclave of 1549 things had become very slack, as attested by a letter written on 5 December by the representative of the Gonzaga family, the ruling house of Mantua:

The cardinals are now on the one-dish regimen. The dish consists of a couple of capons, a nice piece of veal, some salami, a nice soup, and anything you want as long as it is boiled. That is in the morning. Then in the evening, you can have anything you want as long as it is roasted, as well as some antipasti, a main course, some salad and a dessert. The more small-minded ones are complaining about the hardship . . .

Sitting in such comfort, the conclave – split between the supporters of France, the Habsburgs and the late pope – took from 29 November 1549 to 7 February of the following year to elect Cardinal Giovan Maria del Monte as Pope Julius III. As a younger man, del Monte had allegedly fathered over a hundred illegitimate children, but then, on being admonished by his mother, swore he would thenceforward abjure the company of women and stick to boys. He was as good as his word, and on becoming pope presented a cardinal's red hat to his 17-year-old male lover, a monkey trainer by trade.

It was for Pope Julius III, whose health had been sapped by excessive eating, that the celebrated chef Bartolomeo Scappi created his 'royal white tart', made from *provatura* cheese, fine sugar, rosewater, cream and egg whites –plain fare for a sickly pontiff.

1284

The Origin of Tapas Alfonso X 'the Wise', king of Castile, León and Galicia died on 4 April. Tradition has it that when, at some point during his reign, he became ill, his physician advised him to eat snacks between meals to help soak up the wine that he was constantly imbibing. Feeling the benefit of this regime, Alfonso instituted a law that dictated that tavern-keepers could not serve wine to their customers without also providing them with a little something to eat with each glass. *Tapa* literally means 'lid' or 'cover', and it has been suggested that the original tapas were slices of bread, ham or chorizo that drinkers in Andalusia placed over their glasses to keep the flies off their sherry.

1290

Avoid Scratching One's Foul Parts at Table Bearing in mind that at medieval feasts, guests would often help themselves with their fingers from common bowls, Bonvesin de la Riva of Milan gave readers of his *Fifty Courtesies at Table* the following tips on etiquette (the original was in verse):

Thou must not put either thy fingers into thine ears, or thy hands to thy head. The man who is eating must not be cleaning by scraping with his fingers at any foul part.

Bonvesin also advised against sneezing onto one's plate, failing to wipe one's mouth before taking a sip of wine, or sheathing one's knife (everybody had to bring their own to table) before others had finished eating.

The following century a German writer on table manners gave some further advice:

If it happens that you cannot help scratching, then courteously take a portion of your dress and scratch with that. That is more befitting than that your skin should become soiled.

Another medieval authority on etiquette admonished his readers thus:

Let not thy privy members be laid open to be viewed,
It is most shameful and abhorred, detestable and rude.

circa 1300

The Water of Life The Catalan alchemist, astrologer and

physician Arnaldus de Villa Nova recommended eau de vie – a clear fruit brandy – be taken for medicinal purposes: 'Eau de vie prolongs good health, dissipates the humours, rejuvenates the heart and preserves youth.' The clue is in the name: *eau de vie* is French for 'water of life', the same meaning as the Latin *aqua vitae* (once applied to any concentrated solution of alcohol), the Scandinavian caraway- or dill-flavoured spirit *akvavit*, and the Gaelic *usquebaugh*, from which comes the word 'whisky'. Medieval physicians recommended moderation, however: in France, the suggested dose was one tablespoon of eau de vie a day.

1312

Gaveston's Fork A group of barons seized Piers Gaveston, the Gascon favourite of Edward II of England, and put him to death. Gaveston and Edward may or may not have been lovers, but it was taken as a token of the former's effeteness that a table fork was found among his possessions after his death. By this time, forks had been used in Italy for at least two centuries (essential for eating pasta), but did not come into general use in England and the rest of northern Europe until the later 17th century – the century before, Martin Luther had articulated the suspicion that most northerners felt for such decadent innovations when he supposedly declared 'God protect me from forks.' The fork was still very much a novelty to the English traveller Thomas Coryate when he visited Italy, as recorded in *Coryate's Crudities hastily gobbled up in Five Months' Travels in France, Italy, &c.* (1611):

> The Italian, and also most strangers that are commorant in Italy, do always at their meals use a little fork, when they cut their meat. For while with their knife which they hold in one hand they cut the meat out of the dish, they fasten their fork, which they hold in their other hand, upon the same dish, so that whatsoever he be that sitting in the company of any others at meal, should unadvisedly touch the dish of meat with his fingers, from which all at the table do cut, he will give occasion of offence unto the company, as having transgressed the laws of good manners . . .

Coryate himself was credited with introducing the fork to England, and was as a consequence nicknamed *Furcifer*, the Latin for 'fork-bearer' (and also 'rascal'). At first the English fork only had two tines, but the increasing tendency of English cuisine to smaller and daintier morsels led to the necessity of adding a third tine.

1341

The Boar's Head Feast The Queen's College at Oxford was founded by Robert de Eglesfield, chaplain to Philippa of Hainault, queen consort of Edward III. One of the college's more celebrated traditions is the annual Boar's Head Gaudy, a feast held at Christmastime, and said by William Henry Husk, in his *Songs of the Nativity Being Christmas Carols, Ancient and Modern* (1868) to be:

> . . . a commemoration of an act of valour performed by a student of the college, who, while walking in the neighbouring forest of Shotover and reading Aristotle, was suddenly attacked by a wild boar. The furious beast came open-mouthed upon the youth, who, however, very courageously, and with a happy presence of mind, thrust the volume he was reading down the boar's throat, crying, '*Græcum est*,' [with the compliments of the Greeks] and fairly choked the savage with the sage.

At The Queen's College feast, a boar's head is brought into the hall, with a solo singer and choir singing the Boar's Head Carol. Many other places hold Boar's Head Feasts at Christmas, a tradition going back to the pagan Norse, who would sacrifice a boar to the goddess Freyja at the winter solstice. This is thought to be the origin of the traditional ham that many families still eat alongside their turkey at Christmas.

1346

From Poor Knights to Eggy Bread After the Battle of Crécy, many English knights who had been captured by the French were obliged to sell their estates to raise the ransom demanded for their release. Returning home in penury, they were given a pension and living quarters at Windsor Castle by Edward III, who established for them a new chivalric order called the Poor Knights of Windsor. By a process that remains obscure, this name also came to be applied to what the Germans call *arme Ritter* ('poor knights') and the English call French toast (known as German toast until the First World War, and then patriotically renamed in honour of Britain's principal ally in the conflict). The earliest recorded use of the English term 'poor knights' for French toast dates from 1659 (*see* below). The French themselves call this *pain perdu* ('lost bread'), recognizing that it is the best thing to do with 'lost' (i.e. stale) bread; while under the British Raj in India it was called hurry-scurry or Bombay pudding.

— — —

A Recipe for Poor Knights

The following recipe for 'poor knights' (what we now call French toast or eggy bread) comes from *The Compleat Cook*, an anonymous work published in 1659:

> To make Poor Knights, cut two penny loaves in round slices.
>
> Dip them in half a pint of cream, or fair water, then lay them abroad in a dish, and beat three eggs and grated nutmegs and sugar, beat them with the cream.
>
> Then melt some butter in a frying-pan, and wet the sides of the toast and lay them on the wet side, then pour in the rest upon them, and so fry them.
>
> Serve them in with rosewater, sugar and butter.

— — —

1348

Salmon from the Grave The word 'gravlax' is first mentioned in a record from this year, in the form of a man from Jämtland in central Sweden called Olafauer Gravlax. He presumably made his living by preparing gravlax, a word derived from the Swedish *grav*, 'grave', and *lax*, 'salmon'. Traditionally, gravlax was made by burying salted salmon in a hole in the ground (the *grav*), covering it with birch bark and stones and allowing it to ferment for up to a week, so that the flesh was soft enough to eat raw. Today, gravlax is prepared without burial, the salmon being divided into two fillets; one is placed in a dish skin side down, scattered with dill, salt, sugar and white peppercorns; then the other fillet is placed on top of the first, skin side up, and then covered with a weighted board. Every few hours the fillets are turned and basted in the expressed juices; the gravlax is ready in three days.

1350

Reheated Pies and Plagues of Flies In London, a bye-law forbade cookshops from charging more than a penny for a rabbit pasty. Other regulations included bans on buying meat more than a day old, and a prohibition on the reheating of pies – a stipulation ignored by Roger, the eponymous cookshop proprietor of Chaucer's 'Cook's Tale'. In the Prologue to this unfinished story from the *Canterbury Tales*, the Host berates Roger for serving up reheated Jack-of-Dover (a kind of pie, or possibly a fish):

> Now telle on, Roger; looke that it be good,
> For many a pastee hastow laten blood,

And many a Jakke of Dovere hastow soold
That hath been twies hoot and twies coold.
Of many a pilgrym hastow Cristes curs,
For of thy percely yet they fare the wors,
That they han eten with thy stubbel goos,
For in thy shoppe is many a flye loos.

[Now tell on, Roger; look that it be good,
For of many a pastry hast thou drawn out the gravy,
And many a Jack of Dover hast thou sold
That has been twice hot and twice cold.
Of many a pilgrim hast thou Christ's curse,
For of thy parsley yet they fare the worse,
Which they have eaten with thy stubble-fed goose,
For in thy shop is many a fly loose.]

The Parmesan Mountain In the collection of tales known as *The Decameron*, the Italian writer Giovanni Boccaccio conjured up a particularly Italianate Land of Plenty:

There is a mountain made entirely of grated Parmesan. Standing at the top of it are people who do nothing else but make macaroni and ravioli, cook them in capon broth, and then throw them down the slopes. The more you take the more you get.

Parmesan cheese was first mentioned in the 13th century by a monk in Parma called Adamo Salimbene, and by 1568 a Dominican called Bartolomeo Scappi was declaring in his cookbook that Parmesan was the finest cheese in the world. This was a verdict shared by Samuel Pepys, who, during the Great Fire of London in 1666, buried his Parmesan cheese together with his wine and other valuables in order to preserve them from the flames. The cheese's high reputation continues, and a recent survey showed that chunks of Parmesan are the most frequently shoplifted items in Italian supermarkets.

1357

Pardoned for Fasting In his *Book of Days* (1862–4), Robert Chambers gives the following account of a remarkable fast:

In *Rymer's Faedera*, there is a rescript of King Edward III, having reference to a woman named Cecilia, the wife of John de Rygeway, who had been put up in Nottingham gaol for the murder of her husband, and there had remained mute and abstinent from meat and drink for forty days, as had been represented to the king on fully trustworthy testimony; for which reason, moved by piety, and for the glory of God and the Blessed Virgin, to whom the miracle was owing, his grace was pleased to grant the woman a pardon. The order bears date the 25th of April, in the 31st year of the king's reign, equivalent to AD 1357.

circa 1390

Swan Served in its Own Blood 'A fat swan loved he best of any roost.' So wrote Chaucer of his Monk in the *Canterbury Tales*, indicating that this man of God liked his luxuries – for swan was the most expensive bird to eat in the Middle Ages. The preferred mode of serving swan was with a black sauce made from the bird's own finely chopped guts cooked in its blood. To reduce the 'fishy' taste of the meat, the birds were sometimes fed with oats prior to slaughter.

A Coq d'Or on a Gilded Pig

The French royal cook Guillaume Tirel (circa 1310–95), known as Taillevent, is credited with compiling a collection of recipes called *Le Viandier*, the earliest manuscript of which dates from 1395. Presentation and dramatic impact were often as important as taste, as attested by the following 'gilded dish', a 'subtlety' intended for a feast day.

Helmeted Cocks

Roast some pigs, and poultry such as cocks
and old hens.

When the pig is roasted on the one hand, and the chicken on the other, stuff the chicken (without skinning it, if you wish), and [glaze] it with beaten egg batter.

When it is glazed, set it riding on the pig with a helm of glued paper, and with a lance fixed at the breast of the chicken.

Cover them with gold or silver leaf for the lords,
or with white, red or green tin leaf
[for those of lower rank].

THE 15TH CENTURY

circa 1400

Thousand-Year-Old Eggs The origin of this Chinese delicacy, also known as century eggs, is said to go back six centuries to the Ming Dynasty, when, according to legend, a man in Hunan province found some two-month-old duck eggs in some slaked lime that was being used as mortar in the construction of his new home. Curious, the man decided to taste them, and liked what he tasted – especially with the addition of some salt. Today, thousand-year-old eggs are prepared by wrapping them in clay mixed with quicklime, wood ash and salt, and leaving them for several months. At the end of the process, the white is transformed into a dark brown, translucent, virtually tasteless jelly, while the yolk becomes dark green or grey in colour, with a creamy texture and the smell of sulphur or ammonia. This latter characteristic led to the common misconception that thousand-year-old eggs are prepared by being immersed in urine, and indeed the Thais call them *khai yiow ma* – 'horse-piss eggs'.

circa 1450

The Power of Paan The Persian ambassador to the King of Vijayanagara in southern India believed that the king's ability to maintain a harem of several hundred princesses and concubines was largely attributable to his passion for chewing paan – still a widespread habit in India. Paan consists of an areca nut (representing the male principle) with some lime and spices wrapped in a betel leaf (representing the female principle), and is largely chewed to cleanse the palate, freshen the breath and ease the digestion. Chewers expectorate blood-red spit with unsettling frequency, acquire blackened teeth, and are liable to an increased risk of developing mouth cancer.

1453

A Stolen Pleasure Following the fall of Constantinople and the conquest of Greece by the Ottoman Turks, many Greeks, rather than submitting to the foreign yoke, took to brigandage in the mountains. These guerrillas-cum-bandits were known as *klephts*, a word derived from Greek *kleptein*, 'to steal', which is also the root of our word 'kleptomania'. To sustain themselves, the *klephts* stole sheep, which they would cook slowly in pit-ovens, a method that produced very little smoke – which might give away their hiding places to Ottoman soldiers. Thus was born that traditional Greek dish, *kleftiko* – lamb marinated in garlic and lemon juice, then slow-baked on the bone.

An Archiepiscopal Feast

The installation of George Neville as Archbishop of York in 1465 was celebrated by great feasting, the menus for which were recorded in *A Noble Boke of Cokery*, a manuscript compiled in 1468 and which in 1500 became what is probably the first printed cookery book in English. A modest selection of items from the first feast follows:

The First Course

Brawn with Mustard – Frumenty with Venison –
Pheasants – Swan Roast – Gannets – Gulls – Capon –
Heron Roast – Pike – Fritters – Custards

The Second Course

Venison – Peacock – Coney Roast – Woodcock – Plover
– Godwits – Redshanks – Knots – Oxen – Cream in
purple – Tart in mould

The Third Course

Dates in comfit – Bittern roasted – Curlew roasted –
Pheasant roasted – Rails roast – Egrets roast –
Rabbits – Quails – Dotterels roast – Martins roast –
Great birds – Larks roast – Sparrows – Fresh sturgeon
– Quinces baked

To Conclude

Cream – Potages – Pike – Lamprey – Salmon – Gurnard
– Sole – Eels roast – Trout – Perch – Flounders – Shrimps
– Crabs – Lobsters

✺ ✺ ✺

1465

In Taste Alone We Are Undefeated The Italian humanist Bartolomeo Platina, a member of the Roman Academy, wrote *De honesta voluptate et valetudine* ('On Honourable Pleasure and Health'), a work that combines ancient learning and moral philosophy with recipes for fine dining, largely borrowed from the esteemed chef Martino de' Rossi, also known as Maestro Martino of Como. Platina's work was published in 1470, making it the first printed cookbook.

Whereas most Renaissance humanists looked back to the achievements of the ancients in the arts and philosophy as things to be aspired to but not surpassed, Platina makes an exception for 'modern' gastronomy, declaring: 'There is no reason why we should prefer our ancestors' tastes to our own. Even if they surpassed us in nearly all the arts, in taste alone we are undefeated.' What prompts him to make this boast is Maestro Martino's recipe for *biancomangiare* ('white eating', i.e. blancmange), which so delights the author that he cannot contain himself: 'O immortal gods!

What a cook you gave us in my friend Martino of Como!'

Among the other pieces of advice offered by Platina is that there are few dishes that cannot be improved by the addition of sugar, and that roast bear meat is not good for the liver or spleen – but it can forestall baldness.

In 1468, three years after writing his book, Platina and other members of the Academy were arrested, accused of plotting to assassinate Pope Paul II, and furthermore charged with denying God and worshipping instead the deities of ancient Rome. In addition, they were accused of gluttony (the manuscript of Platina's book was taken as evidence) and of sexual incontinence with both men and women. Whether or not there really was any conspiracy against the pope is unknown, but Platina and his friends, after suffering various tortures, were eventually released. Pope Paul's successor, Sixtus VI, later made Platina librarian to the Vatican – an event celebrated in a famous fresco by Melozzo da Forlì.

Vainglorious Peacock

In *De honesta voluptate et valetudine* ('On Honourable Pleasure and Health', 1465), Bartolomeo Platina warns against the eating of peacocks, as they are difficult to digest and induce melancholy. What is more, the peacock is a vainglorious bird eaten by vainglorious people, whose wealth is due to 'mere luck and other people's stupidity', and who would otherwise be stuffing their faces in cheap taverns and brothels along with the other riff-raff. Platina's purpose is above all a moral one – to understand the perfect balance between pleasure and self-restraint. However, he wants to have his cake and eat it too – or his peacock anyway, as he gives detailed instructions about how to make the best impression with the vainglorious bird:

First you must make a shallow cut from the peacock's throat to its tail.

Then peel off the skin, feathers, head and legs.

The body is then stuffed and roasted on a spit.

When it is cooked, it is dressed again in its skin and feathers, and its head and legs restored, and the whole thing wired and nailed together on a platter prior to serving.

For an added flourish, place some wool soaked with camphor in its bill and set light to it as it is brought to the table.

Presumably one's vainglorious guests will be delighted with this ostentatious show.

1471

Death by Melon Pope Paul II died on 26 July. The Italian humanist Bartolomeo Platina, who had spent a year in confinement and suffered torture on Paul's orders (*see* 1465), exacted his revenge when writing his *Lives of the Popes* (1479):

> Paul II loved to have a great variety of dishes at his table, and generally ate of the worst; but he would be vociferous if what he liked were not provided. He loved melons, crabs, sweetmeats, fish and bacon. This odd kind of diet, I believe, caused the apoplexy of which he died; for the day before his death he had eaten two very large melons.

1475

The Origin of Atholl Brose The celebrated Scottish desert, made from oatmeal, honey and whisky, is said to have originated during the rebellion against King James III by John MacDonald, Earl of Ross and Lord of the Isles. In order to capture this rebel earl, the loyal Earl of Atholl filled a small well in Skye with honey and whisky. The Earl of Ross fell for it, and spent many a happy hour supping at this new delight, becoming so inebriated that he was easily captured. However, he escaped retribution for his treason, and lived until 1503.

Another less likely story says the dish originated during the 1745 rebellion of Bonnie Prince Charlie, when the Duke of Atholl, a loyal Hanoverian, used the same ruse to capture some of his Jacobite enemies. The delicious reputation of Atholl brose gave the English poet Thomas Hood the opportunity for a pun:

> Charm'd with a drink which Highlanders compose,
> A German traveller exclaim'd with glee, –
> Potzausend! sare, if dis is Athol Brose,
> How goot dere Athol Boetry must be!

1492

The European Discovery of Chilli When Columbus landed in the Caribbean, he was so convinced that he had reached the East Indies that he named the hot spice he found there 'pepper of the Indies'. In fact, it was the fruit of plants of the genus *Capsicum*, which is native to the New World, and which had been cultivated by native peoples there since around 4000 BC. The confusion has persisted, which is why we call this fruit 'chilli pepper', although it is not related to pepper proper, which comes from various Old World species of the genus *Piper*.

THE 16TH CENTURY

circa 1500

The Butter Tower Work started on the construction of Rouen Cathedral's Tour de Beurre ('Butter Tower'). The tower is so named because the building work was funded by donations from those Normans who wished for a dispensation from the Church so that they could continue to eat butter – the pride of Norman cuisine – throughout Lent.

1505

Chillies to India The Portuguese established their first colony in India at Cochin (now Kochi), and five years later established a settlement at Goa. Although today Indian cuisine is associated above all with the fiery flavour of chillies, prior to the arrival of the Portuguese this spice from the Americas was unknown in India, where hitherto the hottest ingredient had been pepper. Other New World ingredients introduced by the Portuguese to India include papayas, guavas and pineapples, all of which were enthusiastically embraced into Indian cuisine. However, although the Portuguese also introduced tomatoes and potatoes from the Americas, they did not become popular until the time of the British Raj.

Vindaloo: a Portuguese Kárhí

Vindaloo, known today as one of the hottest of curries, originated in the Portuguese colony of Goa. Rather than being a native Indian dish, however, it owes its name and nature to the Portuguese dish called *carne de vinha d'alhos*, composed (as the name suggests) of meat, wine and garlic. These items are also – with the addition of spices and the substitution of vinegar for wine – the leading ingredients of vindaloo. The first recorded mention of the latter word in English is in W.H. Dawe's *Wife's Help to Indian Cookery* (1888), where vindaloo is described as 'a Portuguese Kárhí'. Here is Dawe's recipe:

The following ingredients are employed . . .

Ghee, six chittacks [one chittack = one ounce / 28 grams], lard or oil may be used; garlic ground, one tablespoonful; garlic bruised, one tablespoonful; ginger ground, one tablespoonful; chillies, ground, two teaspoonful; coriander-seed, one teaspoonful; coriander-seed, roasted and ground, half a teaspoonful; bay leaves, or Tej-path, two or three; peppercorns, quarter-chittack; cloves, half a dozen roasted and ground; cardamoms, half a dozen roasted and ground;

cinnamon, half a dozen sticks;
vinegar, quarter-pint

Take a seer [approximately two pounds / one kilogram]
of beef or pork, and cut it into large square pieces,
and steep them in vinegar with salt and the ground
condiments given above, for a whole night.

Warm the ghee, lard, or mustard-oil, with the ingredients
in which it has been soaking overnight and add the
meat with peppercorns and bay leaves, and allow the
whole to simmer slowly over a gentle fire for a couple of
hours, or until the meat is quite tender.

(Dawe's advises that if one is using pork rather than
beef, one should omit the cloves, cardamoms, and
cinnamon.)

1510

Cornish Pasty Originates in Devon Shock In 2006 Dr
Todd Gray, chairman of the Friends of Devon's Archives,
found among the accounts of the Edgecumbe estate in
Devon a recipe for what appears to be a 'Cornish' pasty,
featuring flour, pepper and venison. The manuscript
uncovered by Dr Gray dates from 1510, 236 years before
the first known Cornish recipe for the pasty, dated 1746.

Supporters of the Cornish origin of the pasty, however, point to the 12th-century Arthurian romance *Eric and Enide* by Chrétien de Troyes, which contains the following passage: 'Next Guivret opened a chest and took out two pasties. "My friend," says he, "now try a little of these cold pasties . . ."' As both Guivret and Eric are generally identified as coming from Cornwall, this is said to justify the Cornish claim.

Certainly by the 19th century, the pasty was well established in Cornwall as the 'packed lunch' of the county's tin miners. The way the pastry case — enclosing a filling of diced steak and vegetables — was crimped together meant that the miners could hold the pasty in their dirty fingers by this thick crust and then throw it away after eating the rest of the pasty.

In 2011 the EU awarded the Cornish pasty Protected Geographical Indication (PGI) status, placing it alongside such foods as Parma ham and Camembert cheese. According to the decree, to earn its name, a Cornish pasty should not only be prepared in Cornwall but should also be formed in a D-shape, with the crimp along the side not the top. The contents must be 'chunky', consisting of 'mince or chunks of beef with swede, potato and onion and a light seasoning'. It is doubtful whether the pasty featured in a 1940s playground chant would have passed muster with the EU:

Matthew, Mark, Luke and John
Ate a pasty five feet long.
Ate it once, ate it twice,
Oh my Lord, it's full of mice.

1518

From Panettone to Baba The Italian noblewoman Bona Sforza married Sigismund I 'the Old', and so became Queen of Poland and Grand Duchess of Lithuania. It is thought that she brought with her the recipe for *panettone*, a speciality of her native Milan, and that this gave rise to the Slavic speciality *baba*. This sweetened bread, baked in upright cylindrical moulds, is of such delicacy that it was said the dough needed to rest on eiderdown in a male-free kitchen before being committed to the oven – and no one present was allowed to speak above a whisper. Although the recipe may have been an import, the harvest-time tradition of baking tall cylindrical breads, some of them almost as tall as a human being, goes back to the earlier Middle Ages, when the Slavs were still pagan. The word *baba* itself means 'grandmother', referring to the human-like shape of the cylinders.

1526

Emperor Regrets Conquest on Gastronomic Grounds
Babur, the first Mughal emperor, invaded northern India

but was not best pleased with his conquest. 'Hindustan is a place of little charm,' he complained in his memoirs, the *Baburnama*, adding, 'The cities and provinces are all unpleasant.' The worst thing was the food, so different from that of his homeland in Central Asia: 'There is no good meat, grapes, melons or other fruit. There is no ice, cold water, bread or any good food in the markets.' Late in his reign, Babur's horticulturalists did manage to grow grapes and melons in India, but the taste of the latter made Babur weep for home.

Despite his dislike of Indian food, Babur did employ some Hindustani cooks from the kitchens of the Sultan of Delhi, whom he had recently overthrown. This was a decision he came to regret, for after one meal he began to be violently sick and, suspecting he had been poisoned, he ordered a dog be brought to eat his vomit. The dog soon fell ill, and quickly died. Babur himself recovered, but it transpired that the mother of the deposed sultan had paid one of the cooks to poison the meat. The cook was tortured into a confession, then flayed alive, while the emperor's taster was chopped up into small pieces for having failed in his duties. The sultan's mother was merely put in prison.

1527

The Shock of Bread and Garlic In May, while German mercenaries sacked Rome, Isabella d'Este, Marchioness of

Mantua, found herself besieged in her house for eight days. She later related how she was obliged to subsist on a pauper's diet of bread and garlic, a shock from which she claimed never to have recovered.

- - -

A Renaissance Banquet

On 24 January 1529 Cristoforo Messisbugo, steward to Alfonso I d'Este, Duke of Ferrara, organized one of the most spectacular banquets of the Renaissance, as recorded in his own book *Banchetti composizioni di vivande*, written just before his death in 1548. The feast was to mark the marriage of Alfonso's heir, Ercole d'Este, to Renée, daughter of King Louis XII of France, and marked the climax of eight weeks of celebrations.

In a carefully choreographed sequence, some fifty different dishes, arranged into five courses, were brought to the table, which, in homage to the bridegroom, was adorned with sugar statues depicting the Labours of Hercules. As the hundred or so guests made their way laboriously through the weighty cornucopia, they were diverted by clown shows, comic dialogues, and madrigals and other musical entertainments.

The vast majority of the dishes comprised meat

or fish, many prepared with raisins, cloves, cinnamon, pepper, nutmeg, sugar, eggs, cheese and wine. Here are a few selections from the menu:

Boar rissoles

Pork liver sausages in a pastry case

Boned capon covered in blancmange

Capon livers in caul

Roast pheasant with oranges

Roast francolins

Pigeons in puff pastry

Fried bone-marrow pastries

Whole roasted stuffed goats

Gilded and soused sea bream garnished with laurel leaves

Smoked grey mullet

Fish-spleen tarts

Fried trout tails

Eel in marzipan

Trout-roe pies

Roast lamprey in its own sauce

Salted pike in yellow imperial sauce

Fried turbot covered in sauces in the d'Este colours of
red, white and green

It might have come as some relief to the guests that
Lent began shortly afterwards.

Alfonso's extravagance was, however, all in vain.
In allying his family with the French royal house,
he had backed the wrong horse – after the marriage,
French power in Italy rapidly waned, to the benefit
of the Habsburgs in the person of Emperor Charles
V. By the end of the year, Alfonso was obliged to
pay homage to Charles in Bologna. The duke took
Messisbugo, his head-chef-cum-courtier, with him to
ease the negotiations by pleasing the emperor with
some further banquets, and so impressed was Charles
that he made the steward a count.

- - -

1533

Provoking Venus with an Artichoke Catherine de' Medici
married the future King Henry II of France, and from her
native Italy brought with her a culinary innovation: the

globe artichoke. This had been long regarded as a foodstuff that 'provokes Venus', and was thus thought unsuitable fare for well-brought-up young ladies – causing Parisian greengrocers to hawk their wares with cries of:

> Artichokes! Artichokes! Heats the body *and* the spirit! Warms up your parts! That Catherine de' Medici? She loved her artichokes! Artichokes! Artichokes!

1536

A Lutheran Stomach The Dutch humanist scholar Desiderius Erasmus died. Erasmus had spent his life urging reform of the Roman Catholic Church while refusing to go over to Protestantism. Once, when criticized for failing to observe the Lenten fast, he responded, 'I may have a Catholic soul, but my stomach is Lutheran!'

1539

Jack Horner and the Plum Among the foundations disestablished during Henry VIII's dissolution of the monasteries was the Abbey of Glastonbury. Prior to this, tradition has it that Richard Whiting, the last abbot of Glastonbury, attempted to forestall disaster by sending his steward, Jack Horner, to London with a Christmas gift for the king: a pie in which were hidden the title deeds of 12 manors. On the journey, it is said, Jack Horner opened the pie and extracted the deeds of the manor of Mells for himself – hence the rhyme:

> Little Jack Horner
> Sat in the corner
> Eating a Christmas pie.
> He put in his thumb
> And pulled out a plum
> And said, 'What a good boy am I!'

What is known for certain is that a *Thomas* Horner did take up residence in Mells shortly after the dissolution. But his descendants point out that his first name was Thomas, not Jack, and that he bought the manor (together with some other manors and neighbouring farms) for £1831. 9s. 1¾d. *Jack* Horner, on the other hand, appears to have been a fictional creation, a 13-inch-high prankster whose escapades featured in many 18th-century chapbooks.

1542

Figs Encourage Lice Andrew Boorde published *A Dyetary of Helth*, in which he expiates on the health benefits or

otherwise of a range of foods. Figs may act as an aphrodisiac, he says, but they also 'provoke a man to sweate; wherefore they doth engender lyce'. As for lettuce, it 'doth extynct veneryous actes'. As a young man Boorde had been admitted to the Carthusian order, but in 1529 was freed from his monastic vows, as he found himself unable to endure 'the rugorosite off your relygyon'. He subsequently studied medicine abroad, and travelled widely in Europe, sending back from Catalonia the seeds of rhubarb – a plant then unknown in England. On returning home, he was convicted of keeping three 'loose women' in his house, and seems to have spent some time in prison as a consequence.

1545

British Food Part One: Insatiable Flesh-Eaters In his account of his travels, Nicander Nucius of Corcyra described the English as 'Flesh-eaters, and insatiable of animal food; sottish and unrestrained in their appetites; full of suspicion.'

circa 1550

Seagulls One of the more expensive delicacies in Tudor England were seagulls (also known as mews), which cost five shillings each; in contrast, beef was only a penny half-penny per pound. Between capture and slaughter, the birds were fattened up with salt beef, to enhance the flavour.

1554

Artists' Feasts The Florentine painter and sculptor Giovanni Francesco Rustici died. In a chapter on Rustici in *Lives of the Artists*, his contemporary Giorgio Vasari tells us that Rustici played master of ceremonies in the Company of the Saucepan, a dining club whose members were mostly artists:

One evening when Rustici was giving a supper to his Company of the Saucepan, he ordered that, instead of a table, a great kettle or saucepan should be made out of a wine vat, and they all sat inside it, and it was lighted from the handle which was over their heads. And when they were all comfortably settled, there rose up in the middle a tree with many branches bearing the supper, that is, the food on plates . . . Rustici's dish that time was a cauldron made of pastry, in which Ulysses was dipping his father to make him young again. The two figures were capons with their limbs arranged to make them look like men. Andrea del Sarto, who was one of the Company, presented a temple with eight sides, like S. Giovanni, but resting on columns. The pavement was of gelatine, like different coloured mosaics; the pillars, which looked like porphyry, were great sausages, the base and capitals of Parmesan cheese, the cornices of sugar, and the tribunes of marchpane. In the middle was placed the choir desk of cold veal, with a book of macaroni paste, having the letters and notes for singing made with peppercorns, and those who were singing were thrushes with their beaks open and wearing little surplices, and behind these for the bassi were two fat pigeons, with six ortolans for the soprani.

Rustici also played a prominent part in another dining club, the Company of the Trowel:

> On one occasion, under the direction of Bugiardino and Rustici, they all appeared in the dress of masons and labourers, and set to work to build an edifice for the Company with *ricotta* for mortar, cheese for sand. The bricks, carried in baskets and barrows, were loaves of bread and cakes. But their building being pronounced badly done, it was condemned to be pulled down, upon which they threw themselves upon the materials and devoured them all. At the end, when it was time to break up, there came a cleverly managed shower of rain with much thunder, which forced them to leave off work and return home.
>
> Another time Ceres seeking Proserpine came to the members of the Company and prayed them to accompany her to the lower regions. Descending, they found Pluto, who refused to give her up, but invited them to his wedding feast, where all the provisions were in the form of horrid and disgusting animals, snakes, spiders, frogs and scorpions, and such creatures, which being opened contained food of the most delicate kinds.

Rustici seems to have been something of an eccentric. Vasari tells us that he was very fond of animals, keeping as pets an eagle, a crow 'who could say many things as clearly as a human being', and a porcupine 'which was so tame that it went about under the table like a dog, and used to rub itself against people's legs and make them draw back very quickly'. Not a great deal of his artistic work survives.

1564

The Imperial Sausage Large numbers of locally produced sausages were handed out to the people of Frankfurt am Main to celebrate the coronation of Maximilian II as Holy Roman Emperor – a custom that was maintained for subsequent imperial coronations. The recipe for this local speciality may have originated as early as the 13th century, although the city celebrated the 500th anniversary of the frankfurter in 1987. The recipe was taken to Vienna (German *Wien*) by a German butcher called Johann Georg Lahner (1772–1845), who added some beef to the original pork mixture. These Viennese sausages became known as *Wiener* (or, in the USA, 'weenies').

1567

Welsh Rarebit The anonymous *Merry Tales, Wittie Questions and Quicke Answers* includes the following story about the Welsh fondness for a certain dish:

> There was in heaven a great company of Welshmen which with their cracking and babbling troubled all the others. Wherefore God said to Saint Peter that He was weary of them and that He would have them out of heaven . . . Wherefore Saint Peter went out of heaven-gates and cried with a loud voice, '*Caws pob*' – that is as much to say 'roasted cheese' – which thing the Welshmen hearing, ran out of heaven a great pace. And when Saint Peter saw them all out, he suddenly went into heaven and locked the door.

1570

Pizza Before Pizza Bartolomeo Scappi, personal chef to Popes Pius IV and V and the most celebrated cook of the Italian Renaissance, published his five-volume *Opera*. Among many other things, this work contains a recipe for a dish 'that the Neapolitans call pizza'. This turns out to be a sweet pie with a marzipan crust stuffed with crushed almonds, pine nuts, figs, dates, raisins and biscuits. Tomatoes had not yet been introduced to Italy from the New World, and thus the savoury pizza we know today had not yet been born.

circa 1575

How the Turkey Got Its Name The words 'turkey cock' and 'turkey hen' were originally applied to the African guinea fowl, *Numida meleagris*, which was first introduced to England by traders from the Near East, known as 'Turkey merchants' (referring to the country). When English colonists first came across *Meleagris gallopavo*, a similar-looking bird in North America, they called that a turkey too, and the name stuck. The French word for the North American turkey, *dindon*, derives from *coq d'Inde*, 'cock of the Indies' (i.e. the Spanish colonies in the Americas).

circa 1580

The Birth of Brandy It is said that the first brandy came about when some Dutch merchants began to distil wine so that there would be less volume to carry by sea; the idea was that the concentrate would then be diluted when it arrived at its destination. However, they found that the concentrate had a marvellous quality on its own, and began to drink it undiluted.

1581

Carving Considered as a Fine Art A treatise on carving meat and other foodstuffs, *Il trinciante di Vincenzo Cervio*, was published posthumously in Venice, around a year after the death of the author, the celebrated carver Vincenzo Cervio, who spent much of his life in the household of Cardinal Alessandro Farnese. Cervio decried the sensible German mode of carving, in which the meat was fixed to a plate or table while being cut, and extolled instead the virtuoso Italian style, in which the meat was skewered on a fork, then held up in the air for slicing – a method requiring considerable physical dexterity.

1589

A Chicken in Every Peasant's Pot Henri IV became king of France, and made an announcement for which his memory is still treasured in France: 'I want there to be no peasant in my kingdom so poor that he is unable to have a chicken in his pot every Sunday.'

In contrast, in Italy there was an old proverb that stated: 'When the peasant eats a chicken, either the peasant is ill, or the chicken is.' This alludes to the fact that for the Italian peasant, chicken was a rare and costly luxury, usually reserved for the sick. If a peasant *did* manage to eat a chicken, it was likely to be one that had died of some disease. Another old Italian proverb states that 'St Bernard's sauce makes food seem good.' 'St Bernard's sauce' was hunger (although the connection with the saint is obscure).

Henri IV also had a sauce named in his honour. In the 19th century Jules Collette, chef at a restaurant called Le Pavillon Henri IV, invented a new sauce involving butter, vinegar or lemon juice, egg yolk, shallots, and tarragon or chervil. As Henri IV was known as 'Le Béarnais' (he was a native of Béarn, a traditional province in southwest France), Collette called his invention *sauce Béarnaise*.

The Banquet of the Underfed

In response to the famine then gripping northern Italy, in 1590 the popular Bolognese poet and playwright Giulio Cesare Croce wrote *I banchetti di mal cibati* ('The Banquet of the Underfed'), an allegory in which Lady Famine, daughter of Sir Poor Harvest, marries the youthful Master Sterile. At the wedding feast are served a plethora of dishes, such as:

THE BANQUET OF THE UNDERFED

Bee's ribs and kidneys

Braised wasp, served with its gizzard and caul

Broth of grasshopper's lung

Cicada chops

Cockroach belly

Cricket's eye soup

Fly-head pie

Hornet meatballs

Horsefly's tongue pie

Jellied bat's foot

Midge-foot soup

Mole's offal fried in leech fat

Pan-fried fly liver

Relish of snail's horn

Stewed spleen of spring frog

Wren's tripe

Croce himself, a blacksmith by trade, never sought aristocratic patronage, and died in poverty in 1609.

Among his other works was *The True Rule for Staying Thin and Spending Little*, in which he lists the rich foods – capons, pies, macaroni cheese – that are best avoided if one wants to avoid growing plump, full knowing that no one in Bologna *La Grassa* ('the fat'), as the gastronomic capital of Italy had been known since the 13th century, would have any such ambition.

1590

A Use for Potatoes The potato is thought to have been introduced to the British Isles – possibly by Sir Francis Drake – some time between 1588 and 1593. (Its first foothold in Europe was Spain, where it arrived from Peru around 1570.) As well as becoming a staple foodstuff in places such as Ireland and the Highlands and Islands of Scotland, potatoes were valued as a cure for warts. The technique involved cutting a cross in a tuber, then throwing it away, chanting:

> One, two, three,
> Warts go away from me,
> One, two, three, four,
> Never come back no more.

1591

Roll Out the Barrel The first Great Tun of Heidelberg was completed. This vast barrel in Heidelberg Castle was capable of holding some 30,000 litres of wine – nothing compared to the present Great Tun, built in 1751, which is capable of containing 200,000 litres (although it has rarely been used for this purpose). The hatchet marks left by occupying French soldiers trying to get at the wine (which wasn't there) can still be seen.

> Everybody has heard of the great Heidelberg Tun, and most people have seen it, no doubt. It is a wine-cask as big as a cottage, and some traditions say it holds eighteen thousand bottles, and other traditions say it holds eighteen hundred million barrels. I think it likely that one of these statements is a mistake, and the other is a lie. However, the mere matter of capacity is a thing of no sort of consequence, since the cask is empty, and indeed has always been empty, history says. An empty cask the size of a cathedral could excite but little emotion in me.
>
> Mark Twain, *A Tramp Abroad* (1880)

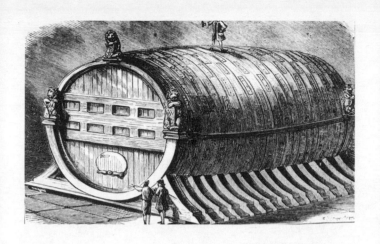

1594

Advice for Modest Drinkers In *The Jewel House of Art and Nature*, the lawyer and horticulturalist Sir Hugh Plat suggested the following method of avoiding total inebriation:

> Drink first a good large draught of salad oil, for that will float upon the wine which you shall drink, and suppress the spirits from ascending into the brain. Also, what quantity soever of new milk you drink first, you may well drink thrice as much wine after, without danger of being drunk. But how sick you shall be with this prevention, I will not here determine, neither would I have set down this experiment, but openly for the help of such modest drinkers as sometimes in company are drawn, or rather forced

to pledge in full bolls such quaffing companions as they would be loth to offend, and will require reason at their hands as they term it.

1597

Brown Bastard In Shakespeare's *Henry IV, Part 1*, Act II, Scene iv, Prince Hal declares, 'Brown bastard is your only drink.' This requires some explanation. 'Bastard' was a type of sweet Spanish wine, similar in flavour to muscadel, and there were both brown and white varieties ('We shall have all the world drink brown and white bastard', *Measure for Measure*, III. i). The term was first used in this sense in the late 14th century, but quite why is obscure. In the *Anatomy of Melancholy* (1621–51), Robert Burton advised against those of a certain disposition from drinking any 'black wines, over-hot, compound, strong thick drinks, as muscadine, malmsey, alicant, rumney, brown bastard, metheglin, and the like', because they are 'hurtful . . . to such as are hot, or of a sanguine choleric complexion, young or inclined to head-melancholy'.

1598

Curry Enters the Language The word 'curry' comes, via the Portuguese *caril*, from the Tamil word *kari*, meaning a sauce or relish to go with rice. Its first appearance in England, in the form 'carrill', comes in William Phillip's 1598 translation of *Discours of voyages into ye Easte & West Indies* by the Dutch merchant Jan Huyghen van Linschoten: 'Most of their fish is eaten with rice, which they seeth in broth which they put upon the rice, and is somewhat sowre . . . but it tasteth well, and is called Carrill.' The British broadened the meaning of the word to cover any spicy Indian stew with a thick sauce. Although in India all such dishes have their own distinct Indian names, the only distinction the British made at the time of the Raj was between the curries of Madras, Bombay and Bengal. If the curries consumed by the British in India were a far cry from genuine Indian cuisine, then those served back home in Britain were, according to Edmund White, the author of *Indian Cookery* (1845), 'nothing more nor less than a bad stew, rendered the more abominably noxious from the quantity of yellowish green fat which must inevitably float in the dish. It would be ridiculous to call such dishes . . . True Indian Curries.'

THE 17TH CENTURY

circa 1600

The Bitter Invention of Satan Western Europeans were at first suspicious of coffee, a drink associated with Arabs, Turks and other non-Christians. For example, in 1599 the English traveller Sir Anthony Shirley wrote of 'damned infidels drinking a certain liquor, which they do call Caffe'. Around the same time, Pope Clement VIII came under pressure to condemn coffee as the 'bitter invention of Satan' and 'Satan's latest trap to catch Christian souls', partly because it was drunk by Muslims – did not the Turks have a saying that 'Coffee should be as black as Hell, strong as death and sweet as love'? – and partly because coffee was regarded as the antithesis of wine, which in the Eucharist becomes Christ's blood. However, according to the popular story, Clement declared, 'This devil's drink is so delicious, we should cheat the devil by baptizing it.' It is sometimes said that Clement's enthusiasm helped to spread the taste for coffee across Europe.

The Five Nectars of the Gods The word 'punch' – in the sense of the drink made up of alcoholic and non-alcoholic ingredients – entered the English language around this time. One theory as to the origin of the word holds that it derives, via Hindi *panch*, from Sanskrit *pancamrta*, meaning 'five nectars of the gods' (the *amrta* element in the Sanskrit word has the same root as 'ambrosia'), alluding to the five ingredients, originally milk, curd, butter, honey and molasses, which were all regarded as medicaments. By the time the Europeans came to India, *panch* was being drunk for pleasure, and the five ingredients were arrack (palm spirit), rosewater, lemon or lime juice, sugar and spices. An alternative theory holds that punch was served by sailors to their passengers en route to India, being drawn from a 'puncheon' or large barrel. But the *Oxford English Dictionary* will have none of it, stating that 'there is no evidence for this view'.

1605

Sacred Water for the Emperor The Mughal emperor Akbar died. Although a Muslim, Akbar banned the slaughter of cattle in deference to the beliefs of his Hindu subjects, and gave up eating beef himself. He also would not drink anything but the water of the River Ganges, sacred to Hindus, and even when the court was hundreds of miles away from the river he would have the holy water brought to him in sealed jars by relays of runners. The water was cooled by decanting it into bottles, which were placed in tubs of water chilled by the addition of saltpetre. When the court was near the Himalaya, ice was brought down from the mountains.

Later in the century, the French traveller Jean-Baptiste Tavernier noted how drinking Ganges water mixed with wine caused he and his companions 'some internal disturbance' – while his servants who drank it undiluted 'were much more tormented than we were'.

To Boil Pigeons with Rice, on the French Fashion

The following recipe comes from John Murrell's *A Newe Booke of Cookerie*, published in 1615.

Put them to boil, and put into their bellies sweet herbs, *viz.* parsley, tops of young thyme.

Then put them into a pipkin [a small earthenware pot or pan], with as much mutton broth as will cover them, a piece of whole mace, a little whole pepper.

Boil all these together until your pigeons be tender. Then take them off the fire, and scum off the fat clean from the broth, with a spoon, for otherwise it will make it to taste rank.

Put in a piece of sweet butter: season it with uergis [ambergris?], nutmeg, and a little sugar: thicken it with rice.

1617

Unpleasant Side-effects of the Jerusalem Artichoke
The Jerusalem artichoke, a native of North America, was
first introduced to England in this year. Shortly afterwards
the gardener John Goodyear noted a side-effect for which
the vegetable has since become notorious:

> They stir up and cause a filthy loathsome stinking
> wind within the body, thereby causing the belly to
> be much pained and tormented, and are a meat more
> fit for swine than men.

Despite its name, the Jerusalem artichoke has nothing to
do with Jerusalem, and is only distantly related to the globe
artichoke. The name derives from the Italian *girasole arti-
ciocco*, 'sunflower artichoke', the plant being a relative of
the sunflower. The Italian *girasole* (like *tournesoleil*, the
French name for the sunflower), literally means 'turn-sun',
referring to the plant's habit of turning its flower to face
the sun.

1633

Escalation In the anonymous *Philosopher's Banquet* (sometimes attributed to Theobaldus Anguilbertus or to Michael
Scot), we find the following advice:

If leeks you like, but do their smell dislike, eat onions, and you shall not smell like leek. If you of onions would the scent expel, eat garlic that shall drown the onion's smell.

1644

Mince Pies and Plum Pudding Prohibited One of the acts of the Puritan Parliament during the English Civil War was to ban the celebration of Christmas, which they regarded as a Papist rite. Along with an end to special church services, there was a specific prohibition on mince pies and plum pudding (dubbed 'the invention of the Scarlet Whore of Babylon'), leading the contemporary pamphleteer Marchamont Needham to pen the following rhyme:

All plums the Prophets' sons [i.e. the Puritans] defy,
And spice-broths are too hot;
Treason's in a December-pie,
And death within the pot.

Although the celebration of Christmas was permitted once more after the Restoration of Charles II in 1660, the specific ban on mince pies and plum pudding was never repealed – so they are still technically illegal in England and Wales.

circa 1645

Risking Divine Displeasure The great Italian general Raimondo Montecuccoli served the Catholic Habsburgs during the Thirty Years War, but his observance of the 'fish on Friday' rule was not as strict as it might be. One Friday he ordered an omelette, but being hungry, he asked for some bacon to be sliced into it. A thunderstorm came on, and a loud clap was heard just as the dinner was served. The general took up the dish, threw the contents out of the window, and facing the thunder, exclaimed, 'What a lot of noise, for a bacon omelette!'

1650

I'll Grind His Bones To Make My . . . Beer In his unreliable *Brief Lives*, John Aubrey (1626–97) tells the following tale:

> Under the cathedral church in Hereford is the greatest charnel house for bones that ever I saw in England. In AD 1650 there lived amongst those bones a poor old woman that, to help out her fire, did use to mix the deadmen's bones: this was thrift and poverty: but cunning alewives put the ashes of these bones in their ale to make it intoxicating.

1652

The Origins of Luncheon According to the *Oxford English Dictionary*, the word 'luncheon' in the sense of a meal first appeared in print – in the form 'lunching' – in Richard Brome's play *A Mad Couple Well Matched*: 'Noonings, and intermealiary Lunchings.' The dictionary negotiates the delicate niceties of the term in its definition of 'luncheon':

> Originally, a slight repast taken between two of the ordinary meal-times, *esp.* between breakfast and mid-day dinner. The word retains this original application with those who use *dinner* as the name of the mid-day meal; with those who 'dine' in the evening, *luncheon* denotes a meal (understood to be less substantial and less ceremonious than *dinner*) taken usually in the early afternoon. Now somewhat *formal*.

This wasn't the first meaning of 'luncheon', which in the now obsolete sense of 'a thick piece; . . . a hunk', is first recorded in 1580 (in the form 'luncheon' rather than 'lunching', discrediting the popular theory that the former is a corruption of the latter). The shorter and more familiar word 'lunch' only began to be used for the meal in the early decades of the 19th century.

1653

Asparagus an Aphrodisiac Nicholas Culpeper published his *Complete Herbal*, which contains observations on the bodily effects of many foods. For example, 'Asparagus . . . being taken fasting several mornings together, stirreth up bodily lust in man or woman.' As for the peach: 'Venus owns the peach tree.'

1655

An Erroneous History of Sirloin It was Thomas Fuller, in his *Church-History of Britain*, who first told the tale that the word sirloin originated in an incident in which Henry VIII was so impressed by a piece of meat set before him that he drew his sword and knighted it. By 1738 Jonathan Swift, in *A Complete Collection of Genteel and Ingenious Conversation*, was attributing the naming to a later king: 'King James the First, being invited to Dinner by one of his Nobles, and seeing a large Loyn of Beef at his Table, he drew out his Sword, and knighted it.' A century later, it was Charles II who was being credited with the jest. In fact the word sirloin comes from Old French *surloigne*, meaning 'above the loin'. It was said that the cut known as 'baron of beef' was so-called as an extension of the 'Sir Loin' joke, but the *Oxford English Dictionary* maintains that this origin is 'unknown'.

1658

For Medicinal Purposes The great Dutch physician and scientist Franciscus Sylvius became professor of medicine at the University of Leiden. While searching for a less expensive substitute for oil of juniper berries – prescribed by physicians as a diuretic – Sylvius tried distilling the juniper berries with spirits, thereby inadvertently making the first gin. It was not long before Sylvius and his colleagues realized that this new concoction had better uses than helping people to pass water.

1659

A Surfeit of Saffron The Duc de Gramont, Marshal of France, did not take to saffron, that most typical of Spanish ingredients. When he was a guest of the Admiral of Castille he complained:

> The feast was magnificent in the Spanish fashion, that is to say prodigious and nobody could eat it all. I saw seven hundred dishes being served, everything in them was the colour of saffron or golden; then I saw them taken back as they had come.

A Dutch Funeral

When the Dutch innkeeper Gerrit van Uyl died in 1660, he made sure his memory was honoured in his native town of Sloten in Friesland by laying on an exceptionally lavish spread, to which it seems the whole town was invited. Here is the bill of fare:

20 oxheads of French and Rhenish wine

70 half-casks of ale

1100 pounds of meat 'roasted on the Koningsplein'

550 pounds of sirloin

28 breasts of veal

12 whole sheep

18 great venison in white pastry

200 pounds of 'fricadelle' (mince meat)

And, in full abundance, bread, mustard, cheese, butter and tobacco

---

1660

A Good Udder In his diary entry for 11 October, Samuel Pepys recorded that 'Mr Creed and I to the Leg in King Street, to dinner, where he and I and my Will had a good udder to dinner.' The consumption of cow's udder – regarded as a form of tripe – is now a rarity, largely restricted to parts of Yorkshire and Lancashire. To remove the last vestiges of milk, the udder must first be soaked for up to four hours in lukewarm water. It is then simmered in salted water until tender (which may take up to six hours). The smell and texture is said to be reminiscent of ox tongue, although the meat is chewier. The prepared udder may be cut into half-inch slices, dipped in whisked egg and breadcrumbs, then fried until golden brown.

To Make an Olio Podrido

The following recipe comes from *The Accomplisht Cook* (1660) by Robert May, a professional English cook who had worked and studied in France for five years. The term 'olio podrido' is an adaptation of the Spanish term *olla podrida*, which (like the French *pot pourri*), literally means 'rotten pot', and denotes a stew in which the liquid may be served as a soup separately from the solids.

Take a pipkin or pot of some three gallons, fill it with fair
water, and set it over a fire of charcoals, and put in first
your hardest meats, a rump of beef, *Bolonia* sausages,
neat's [cow's] tongues two dry, and two green, boiled
and larded, about two hours after the pot is boiled
and scummed:

But put in more presently after your beef is
scummed, mutton, venison, pork, bacon, all the
aforesaid in gubbins [pieces], as big as a
duck's egg, in equal pieces;

Put in also carrots, turnips, onions, two cabbage, in
good big pieces, as big as your meat, a faggot of
sweet herbs, well bound up, and some whole spinach,
sorrel, borage, endive, marigolds, and other good pot-
herbs a little chopped; and sometimes French barley, or
lupins green or dry.

Then a little before you dish out your olio; put to your
pot, cloves, mace, saffron, &c.

— ~ —

1662

Courage In *The History of the Worthies of England*,
Thomas Fuller writes: 'He was a very valiant man who
first ventured on eating of oysters.'

1664

Brandy vs Gin The Alderman Sir William Cooper died, following a dinner of London's Worshipful Company of Clothworkers. Sir William had drunk copious amounts of the Company's brandy, and his distraught wife blamed his death on the noxious quality of the spirits served up by the Clothworkers. It appeared that by her own death she had at least partly forgiven them, for she left an endowment to provide the Clothworkers in perpetuity with a supply of a spirit she considered much more healthy: gin. To this day, at the Clothworkers' feasts, guests are offered a choice of gin or brandy with the question, 'Do you dine with Alderman or Lady Cooper?'

In Praise of Chestnuts In *Sylva, or a Discourse of Forest Trees*, the diarist John Evelyn promoted a foodstuff much neglected by the English:

> But we give that fruit to our swine in England, which is amongst the delicacies of princes in other countries . . . The best tables in France and Italy make them a service, eating them with salt, in wine or juice of lemon and sugar; being first roasted in embers on the chaplet [gridiron]; and doubtless we might propagate their use amongst our common people, being a food so cheap, and so lasting.

Incidentally, the 'chest' in the word 'chestnut' has nothing to do with chests; rather, it derives from Middle English *chasteine*, itself derived (via Old French *chastaigne*) from Latin *castanea*, 'chestnut', and ultimately from a Greek word meaning 'Castanian nut', referring either to the city of Castania in Pontus (Asia Minor), or to Castana in Thesally.

1665

Onions Ward Off Plague As the Great Plague cut a swathe through the population of London, it was noted that onion-sellers appeared to be immune to the disease. The same phenomenon was remarked upon during the cholera epidemic of 1849.

My Lady of Monmouth's Capon in White-Broth

The following recipe is one of many collected or created by the English diplomat Sir Kenelm Digby (1603–65), and posthumously published in 1669 in *The Closet of the Eminently Learned Sir Kenelm Digby Opened*.

*My Lady of Monmouth boileth a capon with
white-broth thus.*

Make reasonable good broth, with the crag-ends of
necks of mutton and veal (of which you must have so
much as to be at least three quarts of white-broth in the
dish with the capon, when all is done, else it will not
come high enough upon the capon).

Beat a quarter of a pound of blanched almonds with
three or four spoonfuls of cream, and, if you will, a little
rose water; then add some of your broth to it, so to
draw out all their substance, mingling it with the rest of
your broth.

Boil your capon in fair-water by itself; and a marrow-
bone or two by themselves in other water. Likewise some
chess-nuts (instead of which you may use pistachios, or
macerated pine kernels) and in other water some skirrits
[?] or endive, or parsley-roots, according to the season.
Also plumpsome raisins of the sun, and stew some sliced
dates with sugar and water.

When all is ready to join, beat two or three new-laid
eggs (whites and all) with some of the white-broth, that
must then be boiling, and mingle it with the rest, and let
it boil on: and mingle the other prepared things with it,
as also a little sliced oringiado [candied orange peel]
(from which the hard candy-sugar hath been soaked
off with warm water) or a little peel of orange (or some

lemon pickled with sugar and vinegar, such as serves for salets [salads]) which you throw away, after it hath been a while boiled in it: and put a little sack to your broth, and some ambergris, if you will, and a small portion of sugar; and last of all, put in the marrow in lumps that you have knocked out of the boiled bones.

Then lay your capon taken hot from the liquor he is boiled in, upon sippets [small pieces] and slices of toasted light bread, and pour your broth and mixture upon it, and cover it with another dish, and let all stew together a while: then serve it up. You must remember to season your broth in due time with salt and such spices as you like.

~ ~ ~

1668

Tasting the Stars A young Benedictine monk called Dom Pérignon joined the Abbey of Hautvillers, near Épernay in Champagne, and went on to become the abbey's cellar master, a post he held until his death in 1715. Legend has it that it was Dom Pérignon who created the first champagne, by forcing bubbles into white wine. This was not in fact the case, but he did much to enhance the quality of the wines produced by the abbey, improving the naturally bubbly wine, using corks to preserve the bubbles, and blending his grapes to produce a light white, rather than the heavy red traditional to the region. There is a story that when he first tried his new improved wine he exclaimed, 'Come quickly, I am tasting the stars!' Louis XIV became a major fan of Dom Pérignon's new wine, and is said to have been the first to bathe in it – a habit later shared by such stars as Marilyn Monroe and Jayne Mansfield.

Betrayed by a Collation of Sweetmeats Early in her career as a royal mistress, Nell Gwyn was faced with a rival for the favours of Charles II, in the form of another actress, Moll Davis. With the aid of her friend, the playwright Aphra Behn, Miss Gwyn devised a way of dealing once and for all with Miss Davis:

> Nell Gwyn having notice that Miss Davis was to be entertain'd at night, by the King in his bed chamber, she invited the lady to a collation of sweetmeats, which being made up with physical ingredients [i.e. a powerful laxative], the effects thereof had such an operation upon the harlot, when the King was caressing her in bed with the amorous sports of Venus, that a violent and sudden looseness obliging her Ladyship to discharge her artillery, she made the King, as well as herself, in a most lamentable pickle;

which caused her Royal Master to turn her off, with the small pension of a thousand pounds per annum, in consideration for her former services in the affairs of love; after which she never appear'd again at Court.

Captain Alexander Smith, *The School of Venus,
or, Cupid restor'd to Sight: being a history of
Cuckolds and Cuckold-makers* (1716)

A Peck of Snails and a Pint of Earthworms

In 1670 Hannah Wolley, whose *Cooks Guide* of 1664 had made her the first female author of an English-language cookery book, published *The Queenlike Closet*. As well as containing recipes for all kinds of dishes, the latter volume also paid attention to the preparation of medicinal drinks, such as the following:

The Snail Water Excellent for Consumptions.

Take a peck of snails with the shells on their backs, have in a readiness a good fire of charcoal well kindled, make a hole in the midst of the fire, and cast your snails into the fire, renew your fire till the snails are well roasted, then rub them with a clean cloth, till you have rubbed off all the green which will come off.

Then bruise them in a mortar, shells and all, then take clary, celandine, borage, scabious, bugloss, five leav'd grass, and if you find yourself hot, put in some wood-sorrel, of every one of these one handful, with five tops of angelica.

These herbs being all bruised in a mortar, put them in a sweet earthen pot with five quarts of white wine, and two quarts of ale, steep them all night; then put them into an alembic [a type of retort used in distillation], let the herbs be in the bottom of the pot, and the snails upon the herbs, and upon the snails put a pint of earthworms slit and clean washed in white wine, and put upon them four ounces of aniseeds or fennel-seeds well bruised, and five great handfuls of rosemary flowers well picked, two or three races [roots] of turmeric thin sliced, harts-horn and ivory, of each four ounces, well steeped in a quart of white wine till it be like a jelly, then draw it forth with care.

1671

Taking One's Duties Seriously At the Château de Chantilly, Louis de Bourbon, Prince of Condé, played host at a banquet for some 2000 guests, including King Louis XIV. The man in charge of the feasting was the great chef François Vatel. However, Vatel, a stickler for detail, was deeply distressed by a number of mishaps, culminating in the news that the large quantities of fish he had ordered – the banquet was to take place on a Friday – would not arrive in time. Unable to bear the disgrace, Vatel fixed his sword to the door of his chamber and ran himself through. According to one version of the story, the servant who found his body had come to tell him that the fish had safely arrived after all.

1673

What Makes Cheese Green? In his *Observations topographical, moral, and physiological, made on a Journey through part of the Low Countries, Germany, Italy and France*, the English traveller and naturalist John Ray gave a detailed account of the great variety of Dutch cheeses, including a green cheese 'said to be coloured with the juice of sheep's dung'.

1674

The Women's Petition Against Coffee An anonymous pamphlet of this title appeared in England, arguing that the drinking of coffee led people to 'trifle away their time ... and spend their money, all for a little base, black, thick, nasty, bitter, stinking, nauseous puddle of water'. Even in France, that land of coffee drinkers, it was realized that moderation was important – as advised by the renowned gourmet Jean Anthelme Brillat-Savarin, in his *Physiologie du goût* ('Physiology of Taste'; 1825): 'It is the duty of all papas and mamas to forbid their children to drink coffee, unless they want to have little dried-up machines, stunted and old at the age of twenty.'

1678

200 Cuppas a Day In his *Tractaat van het Excellent Kruyd Thee*, the Dutch writer Cornelis Bontekoe suggested that to maintain health one should drink a minimum of 8 to 10 cups of tea per day, and that 50 or even 200 cups would not be excessive. By 1696 a Dutch newspaper, the *Haagsche Mercurius*, was reporting that tea-drinking had so dessicated Bontekoe's 'balsamic sap' that 'his joints rattled like castanets'. But, on the whole, the Dutch were strongly in favour of tea, as the following anonymous rhyme from the 1670s attests:

> Tea that helps our head and heart,
> Tea medicates most every part,
> Tea rejuvenates the very old,
> Tea warms the piss of those who're cold.

1679

Let Them Eat Salmon In *Old Mortality*, Sir Walter Scott's 1816 novel set at the time of the Covenanter Rising of 1679, the author describes how salmon was not always regarded as a luxury:

> A large boiled salmon would now-a-days have indicated a more liberal housekeeping; but at that period salmon was caught in such plenty in the considerable rivers of Scotland, that instead of being accounted a delicacy, it was generally applied to feed the servants, who are said sometimes to have stipulated that they should not be required to eat a food so luscious and surfeiting in its quality above five times a week.

Similar stipulations seem to have prevailed elsewhere. Travelling in the Netherlands in the 1730s, Thomas Nugent reported that 'servants used formerly to make a bargain with their master not to be obliged to eat salmon above twice a week'.

A Digester of Bones The French-born physicist Denis Papin, an associate of the great Robert Boyle, demonstrated his 'New Digester or Invention for Softning Bones' to the Royal Society in London. Pepin used his machine to show that if bones are cooked under pressure for a sufficient length of time, they will produce both marrowfat and a pulp that can be used for thickening sauces. The bones themselves are rendered so brittle that they can easily be ground up into bone-meal. In subsequent versions of the digester, Pepin included a steam-release valve, to stop the device from exploding. Pepin's digester was in effect the first pressure-cooker – and indeed a forerunner of the steam engine, the first version of which was built in 1697 by Thomas Savery, who based it on Pepin's designs.

1683

The Origins of the Croissant – Possibly During the Turkish siege of Vienna, a surprise night-time attack on the city was foiled by a baker, who, up early to fire his oven, heard the sounds of tunnelling underground. He raised the alarm, and the Turkish tunnel was blown up. In celebration, the baker came up with a new pastry, the *kipferl*, which had the shape of a crescent – the symbol of Islam, as featured on the Ottoman flags of the attackers. The *kipferl* quickly became a Viennese speciality.

Attractive though this story is, the existence of the *kipferl* has been documented since at least the 13th century, and crescent-shaped breads (representing the Moon) go back to classical times. Be that as it may, when in the 1830s August Zang, a former Austrian artillery officer, opened his Boulangerie Viennoise in Paris's rue de Richelieu, his *kipferl* were so popular that Parisian bakers attempted to imitate it – and came up with something they called the *croissant* – which literally means 'crescent'.

1685

On the Avoidance of Spitting at Table In the etiquette book entitled *The Rules of Civility; or, Certain Ways of Deportment observed amongst all Persons of Quality upon several Occasions* – the English translation of Antoine de

Courtin's 1671 *Nouveau traité de la civilité* – the less couth diners among us are admonished thus:

> You must forbear hawking and spitting as much as you can, and when you are not able to hold, if you observe it neat and kept cleanly, you must turn your back and rather spit in your handkerchief than the room.

This was obviously a lesson the English found it hard to take on board, as an anonymous writer on etiquette felt obliged in 1730 to remind his readers that 'Coughing, yawning or sneezing over the dishes should be carefully avoided.'

1686

The Staffordshire Wonder Robert Plot, in his *Natural History of Staffordshire*, tells the story of Mary Waughton of Wigginton, who in one day never ate more than 'a piece above the size of half-a-crown in bread and butter; or, if meat, not above the quantity of a pigeon's egg at most.' He goes on:

> She drinks neither wine, ale, or beer, but only water or milk, or both mixed, and of either of these scarce a spoonful in a day. And yet she is a maiden of a

fresh complexion, and healthy enough, very piously disposed, of the Church of England, and therefore the less likely to put a trick upon the world; besides, 'tis very well known to many worthy persons with whom she has lived, that any greater quantities, or different liquors, have always made her sick.

1688

On the Uses of Drunkenness On 12 November Sir George Etheredge, author of *The Man of Mode* and other Restoration comedies, wrote to the Duke of Buckingham that in youth and middle age, drunkenness should be avoided as it only served to diminish one's ardour in the nobler pursuit of love. However:

> In old age . . . when it is convenient to forget and steal from ourselves, I am of opinion that a little drunkenness, discreetly used, may as well contribute to our health of body as tranquillity of soul.

circa 1690

Rancid Fish Puts a Spring in One's Step In his account of life at the Mughal court in India, the Italian traveller Niccolao Manucci describes how the King of Balkh (in what is now northern Afghanistan) sent a hundred camels bearing gifts to the Emperor Aurangzeb. Among the presents were boxes of rancid fish – apparently regarded as just the thing to sharpen declining desire.

— — —

A Remedy for Hangovers

The Irish scientist Robert Boyle (1627–91), formulator of Boyle's law and regarded as the father of modern chemistry, should also be remembered for his 'after drinking cure for the headache':

Take green hemlock that is tender.

Put it in your socks, so that it may lie thinly between them and the soles of your feet.

Shift the herbs once a day.

— — —

1694

Pourquoi Picnique? The year 1694 witnessed the first recorded use of the word 'picnic', in the form of the French phrase *repas à picnique*. Intially a *repas à picnique* was a meal (not necessarily outdoors) at which each diner contributed a share of the food, or paid for their own share.

The word may derive from Middle French *piquer*, 'steal, pilfer', and *nique*, which denoted a small copper coin, hence, figuratively, 'nothing at all'. The word 'picnic' is first recorded in English in 1748, apparently in the context of a meal taken at the card table. Only later, it seems, did picnics move out of doors.

1695

Drinking Each Other's Blood In his *Description of the Western Isles of Scotland*, Martin Martin (himself a native of Skye), described a Hebridean variant on the traditional method of forming a blood-brotherhood:

Their ancient leagues of friendship were ratified by drinking a drop of each other's blood, which was commonly drawn out of the little finger. This bond was religiously observed as a sacred bond; and if any person after such an alliance happened to violate the same, he was from that time reputed unworthy of all honest men's conversation.

1697

The Testicle Fruit The first mention in English of the avocado pear, native to the West Indies, is found in William Dampier's *New Voyage Around the World*, published in 1697. The Spanish word *avocado* ('advocate') is in fact a corruption of the Nahuatl word *ahuácatl*, meaning 'testicle' or 'scrotum' – a reference to the shape of the fruit. A further corruption occurred in the 18th century when some English-speakers began to refer to the 'alligator pear'.

Whence Barbecue? Dampier's *New Voyage* also has the first mention in English of the word 'barbecue', which originally denoted a wooden framework either for sleeping on, or for supporting meat that is to be smoked or dried. It has been widely mooted that the word itself comes from the French *barbe à queue*, 'beard to tail'. However, the *Oxford English Dictionary* dismisses this as 'an absurd conjecture', and states that the word appears to derive from an Amerindian language spoken in Guyana. Whatever its origin, few would disagree with the Italian proverb that maintains that 'Even an old boot tastes good if it is cooked over charcoal.' *Contra* this view, in *Freud on Food* (1978) the British chef and Liberal MP Clement Freud declared: 'To barbecue is a way of life rather than a desirable method of cooking.'

Sin-eating The antiquary and gossip John Aubrey died. Among the many unpublished manuscripts he left behind are a number of accounts of the custom of sin-eating, whereby when someone died, certain professionals would, in return for a fee, ceremonially 'eat' the sins of the deceased, thereby taking the sins upon themselves. The custom may have originally been inspired by a passage in the Old Testament referring to the role of the priests: 'They eat up the sin of my people' (Hosea, 4:8). In one passage Aubrey has this to say:

> Within the memory of our fathers, in Shropshire, in those villages adjoining to Wales, when a person died, there was notice given to an old 'sire' (for so they called him), who presently repaired to the place where the deceased lay, and stood before the door of the house, when some of the family came out and

furnished him with a cricket (or stool), on which he sat down facing the door. Then they gave him a groat, which he put in his pocket; a crust of bread, which he ate; and a full bowl of ale, which he drank off at a draught. After this, he got up from the cricket, and pronounced, with a composed gesture, 'the ease and rest of the soul departed, for which he would pawn his own soul'.

Elsewhere, Aubrey gives this account:

In the county of Hereford was an old custom at funerals to hire poor people, who were to take upon them sins of the party deceased. One of them (he was a long, lean, ugly, lamentable poor rascal), I remember, lived in a cottage on Rosse highway. The manner was, that when the corpse was brought out of the house, and laid on the bier, a loaf of bread was brought out, and delivered to the sin-eater, over the corpse, as also a mazard bowl [drinking vessel], of maple, full of beer (which he was to drink up), and sixpence in money: in consideration whereof he took upon him, ipso facto, all the sins of the defunct, and freed him or her from walking after they were dead.

Elsewhere again, Aubrey states that 'this custom was heretofore used all over Wales' and that in 1686 it was still practised in the north of that country.

〜 〜 〜

Pickled Ash-Keys

In his *Acetaria: A Discourse on Sallets*, published in 1699, the renowned diarist and gardener John Evelyn provided a recipe for pickled ash-keys, the clusters of fruits of the ash tree:

Ashen Keys

Gather them young, and boil them in three or four waters to extract the bitterness;

And when they feel tender, prepare a syrup of sharp white-wine vinegar, sugar, and a little water.

Then boil them on a very quick fire, and they will become a green colour, fit to be potted so soon as cold.

The taste for ash-keys has not persisted into the modern era. As Edward Hulme observed in his *Wild Fruits of the Country-Side* (1902), 'After one's first taste one is not conscious of any special hankering for them.'

〜 〜 〜

THE 18TH CENTURY

1703

The Bland Leading the Bland Louis de Béchamel, Marquis de Nointel and head steward to Louis XIV of France, died. It is thought that it was either the marquis or one of his chefs who came up with a thick white sauce flavoured with onion and seasonings, and it is generally agreed that this – one of the basic sauces of French cuisine – was named in his honour. In the spirit of petty jealousy that dominated court life at Versailles, another noble nonentity, the Duc d'Escars, complained: 'That fellow Béchamel has the luck of the devil. My chef was serving breast of chicken à la crème years before he was even born, but no one bothered to name a sauce after *me*.'

1715

Out of the Ordinary The term 'hors d'oeuvre' was first used in English by Joseph Addison in *The Spectator*, No. 576. Initially the expression denoted, in Addison's words, 'something which is singular in its kind', in other words, out of the ordinary course of things. The phrase was originally French, in which it literally means 'outside [the] work', but from the late 16th century it denoted any small building, such as an outhouse, that was not part of an architect's grand plan. By the 1740s in England the phrase had acquired its modern meaning, something 'out of the ordinary' to stimulate the palate before the main courses are served.

1718

Sheep Poo Banned from Coffee The Irish Parliament passed a law banning the adulteration of coffee beans with sheep droppings. Coffee aficionados, although rejecting sheep or rabbit droppings, are more than happy for their coffee beans to have passed through the digestive system of a civet (*see circa* 1850).

The Manchu Han Imperial Feast

In China in 1720, the so-called Kangxi Emperor, the fourth emperor of the imperial Qing (Manchu) dynasty, held a lavish series of banquets known as the Manchu Han Imperial Feast. The aim was not only to celebrate his 66th birthday, but also to reconcile the native Han Chinese with their Manchu conquerors by celebrating the cuisines of both peoples. The feast was spread over three days and six banquets, and featured over 300 different dishes. Here is just a small sample:

Camel's hump

Monkey's brains

Ape's lips

Leopard foetuses

Rhinoceros tails

Deer tendons

Shark's fins

Dried sea cucumbers

Snowy Palm
(bear claw with sturgeon)

Golden Eyes and Burning Brain
(bean curd simmered in the brains of ducks, chickens
and cuckoos)

The Golden Cordial

The Compleat Housewife, by E. (possibly Eliza) Smith, was first published in London in 1727, and in 1742 it became the first cookery book to be printed in America (in Williamsburg). Among the book's many recipes is this one for the 'Golden Cordial':

Take two gallons of brandy, two drams and a half of double-perfum'd alkermes [a liqueur coloured red by the inclusion of the insect *Kermes vermilio*], a quarter of a dram of oil of cloves, one ounce of spirit of saffron, 3 pound of double-refin'd sugar powder'd, a book of leaf-gold.

First put your brandy into a large new bottle; then put three or four spoonfuls of brandy in a china cup, mix your alkermes in it; then put in your oil of cloves, and mix that, and do the like to the spirit of saffron; then pour into your bottle of brandy, then put in your sugar, and cork your bottle, and tie it down close; shake it well together, and so do every day for two or three days, and let it stand about a fortnight.

You must set the bottle so, that when 'tis rack'd off into other bottles, it must only be gently tilted; put into every bottle two leaves of gold cut small; you may put one or two quarts to the dregs, and it will be good, tho' not so good as the first.

Gold leaf has long been used in recipes, and is entirely harmless; in the EU list of permitted food additives, it is given the designation E175.

1729

A Modest Proposal Jonathan Swift published his savage satire entitled *A Modest Proposal, for preventing the children of poor people in Ireland, from being a burden on their parents or country, and for making them beneficial to the publick*. His proposal is as follows:

I have been assured by a very knowing American of my acquaintance in London, that a young healthy child well-nursed is at a year old a most delicious, nourishing and wholesome food, whether stewed, roasted, baked, or boiled, and I make no doubt that it will equally serve in a fricassee, or a ragout.

I do therefore humbly offer it to public consideration, that of the hundred and twenty thousand children, already computed, twenty thousand may be reserved for breed, whereof only one fourth part to be males; which is more than we allow to sheep, black cattle, or swine, and my reason is, that these children are seldom the fruits of marriage, a circumstance not much regarded by our savages, therefore, one male will be sufficient to serve four females. That the remaining hundred thousand may, at a year old, be offered in sale to the persons of quality and fortune, through the kingdom, always advising the mother to let them suck plentifully in the last month, so as to render them plump, and fat for a good table. A child will make two dishes at an entertainment for friends, and when the family dines alone, the fore or hind quarter will make a reasonable dish, and seasoned with a little pepper or salt, will be very good boiled on the fourth day, especially in winter.

I have reckoned upon a medium, that a child just born will weigh 12 pounds, and in a solar year, if tolerably nursed, encreaseth to 28 pounds.

I grant this food will be somewhat dear, and therefore very proper for landlords, who, as they have already devoured most of the parents, seem to have the best title to the children.

1731

Fish Should Swim Thrice Jonathan Swift completed *A Complete Collection of Genteel and Ingenious Conversation* (published 1738), in which Lord Smart opines that 'Fish should swim thrice,' elaborating that 'first it should swim in the sea . . . then it should swim in butter; and at last, sirrah, it should swim in good claret'.

1735

The Roast Beef of Old England Richard Leveridge penned the music and Henry Fielding the words of 'The

Roast Beef of Old England', a patriotic song that soon became hugely popular, being regularly sung by theatre audiences before and after the play.

> When mighty roast beef was the Englishman's food,
> It ennobled our hearts and enriched our blood,
> Our soldiers were brave and our courtiers were
>   good,
> *O! the Roast Beef of Old England!*
> *And O! for old England's Roast Beef!*

> But since we have learned from all vapouring France,
> To eat their ragouts, as well as to dance.
> We are fed up with nothing but vain Complaisance,
> *Oh! The Roast Beef, &c.*

> Our fathers of old were robust, stout and strong,
> And kept open house, with good cheer all day
>   long,
> Which made their plump tenants rejoice in this
>   song –
> *Oh! The Roast Beef, &c.*

> But now we are dwindled to what shall I name,
> A sneaking poor race, half begotten and tame,
> Who sully those honours that once shone in fame,
> *Oh! The Roast Beef, &c. &c. &c.*

A century and a half later, the tune of Leveridge's song was played by a bugler every evening on board the *Titanic* to summon the first-class passengers to dinner.

In 1748 the artist William Hogarth painted *Oh, The Roast Beef of Old England* (above), in which a side of beef is carried into the port of Calais for the consumption of English tourists, while various weak and scrawny-looking Frenchmen look on with envy. Hogarth had been prompted to paint this patriotic picture by a recent experience in which, while sketching the gate of Calais, he had been arrested by the French authorities and charged with espionage. Luckily for Hogarth, France and Britain were then negotiating a peace agreement, and the painter was merely put on the first ship back to Dover.

In the same year as Hogarth painted his picture, Per Kalm, a Swedish visitor to England, noted:

> The English men understand almost better than any other people the art of properly roasting a joint, which is also not to be wondered at; because the art of cooking as practised by most Englishmen does not extend much beyond roast beef and plum pudding.

Not for nothing, therefore, do the French refer to the English as *les rosbifs* (although, following the behaviour of English football fans in France during the 1998 World Cup, they are now more commonly known as *les fuckoffs*).

~ - ~

Cooking Meat by Necromancy

In 1735 or thereabouts an English actor called John Rich invented a device called the 'necromancer', a type of chafing dish with a closely fitting lid that could rapidly cook thin slices of meat using spills of brown paper as fuel. The 'necromancer' later metamorphosed into the 'conjuror', a description of which is to be found in Eliza Acton's *Modern Cookery for Private Families* (1845):

> Steaks or cutlets may be quickly cooked with a sheet or two of lighted paper only, in the apparatus called a conjuror.

> Lift off the cover and lay in the meat properly seasoned, with a small slice of butter under it, and insert the lighted paper in the aperture shown; in from eight to ten minutes the meat will be done, and found to be remarkably tender, and very palatable: it must be turned and moved occasionally during the process.

> This is an especially convenient mode of cooking for persons whose hours of dining are rendered uncertain by their avocations. The part in which the meat is placed is a block of tin, and fits closely into the stand, which is of sheet iron.

1736

Cuckold's Comfort In Britain the Gin Act imposed high taxes on the increasingly popular spirit, leading to riots in London, Norwich, Bristol and other cities. Retailers, in an effort to circumvent the letter of the law, sold gin under such names as Cuckold's Comfort, Bob, Make Shift, Slappy

Bonita, Madam Geneva, the Ladies' Delight, the Balk, Cholic, Grape Waters, or even King Theodore of Corsica. The authorities were not deceived.

1741

The Effects of Scurvy From the beginnings of the European age of exploration, long sea voyages had been accompanied by a terrible disease: scurvy. At its outset scurvy is characterized by lethargy, spongy gums, spots on the skin and bleeding from the mucous membranes; as the disease takes hold, it is marked by suppurating wounds, loss of teeth, jaundice, fever and death. When Admiral George Anson led his Royal Navy squadron in a circumnavigation of the globe in 1740–4 it was still not understood that scurvy is caused by poor diet, specifically a lack of fresh fruit and vegetables (which we now know contain vitamin C, the absence of which causes scurvy). Anson's chaplain, Richard Walter, in *A Voyage Round the World* (1748), described some of the terrible effects of the disease, which killed two out of every three men on the voyage:

This disease, so frequently attending all long voyages, and so particularly destructive to us, is usually attended with a strange dejection of the spirits, and with shiverings, tremblings, and a disposition to be seized with the most dreadful terrors on the slightest accident. Indeed, it was most remarkable, in all our reiterated experience of this malady, that whatever discouraged our people, or at any time damped their hopes, never failed to add new vigour to the distemper . . .

A most extraordinary circumstance, and what would be scarcely credible upon any single evidence, is, that the scars of wounds which had been for many years healed were forced open again by this virulent distemper. Of this there was a remarkable instance in one of the invalids on board the *Centurion*, who had been wounded above fifty years before at the Battle of the Boyne; for though he was cured soon after, and had continued well for a great number of years past, yet, on his being attacked by the scurvy, his wounds, in the progress of his disease, broke out afresh, and appeared as if they had never been healed.

A naval surgeon called James Lind proved in the 1750s that scurvy could be prevented by the consumption of lime or lemon juice; and Captain James Cook, on his voyages of discovery in the 1760s and 1770s, took along large stores of sauerkraut, which also proved effective. However, it was not until the end of the century that the Royal Navy made concentrated lime juice part of the standard seaman's ration.

1744

Indigestion Versified The Scottish physician John Armstrong put his medical advice into verse in *The Art of Preserving Health*, the second book of which concerns diet and warns against consuming too much oil and fat:

> Th' irresoluble oil,
> So gentle late and blandishing, in floods
> Of rancid bile o'erflows: what tumults hence,
> What horrors rise, were nauseous to relate.
> Choose leaner viands, ye whose jovial make
> Too fast the gummy nutrient imbibes.

1745

Divine Guidance on Eating At the commencement of his mystical career, the Swedish scientist and philosopher Emanuel Swedenborg was in London, as described a century later by Caroline Fox in her journal for 7 April 1847:

Swedenborg . . . went into a little inn in Bishopsgate Street, and was eating his dinner very fast, when he thought he saw in the corner of the room a vision of Jesus Christ, who said to him, 'Eat slower.' This was the beginning of all his visions and mysterious communications.

Other accounts suggest that after finishing his meal, a darkness fell upon Swedenborg's eyes, and he became aware in the corner of the room of a mysterious stranger, who told him 'Do not eat too much.' Terrified, Swedenborg rushed home, only for the stranger to appear again in his dreams, announcing that he was the Lord, and that he had appointed Swedenborg to reveal the spiritual meaning of the Bible. History does not record whether Swedenborg's eating habits were indeed altered by this experience.

1747

How Not to Fry an Egg Hannah Glasse, the anonymous author of *The Art of Cookery Made Plain and Easy, by a Lady*, decried the French method of frying eggs:

> I have heard of a cook that used six pounds of butter to fry twelve eggs, when, everybody knows that understands cooking, that half a pound is full enough.

She goes on to include a recipe on 'How to roast a pound of butter.' Mrs Glasse had no great admiration for French cuisine: after giving detailed instructions on 'the French way of dressing partridges', she concludes, 'This dish I do not recommend; for I think it an odd jumble of trash.' One of her more exotic recipes was for 'Icing a Great Cake Another Way', which involved the use of ambergris, a waxy and highly perfumed secretion from the intestinal tract of the sperm whale. (Incidentally, the Chinese, who sprinkled ambergris into their tea, called the substance 'flavour of dragon's saliva'.)

First Catch Your Hare

These words have long, and erroneously, been supposed to appear in Hannah Glasse's *The Art of Cookery Made Plain and Easy* (1747). Here, to set the record straight, is her recipe for roast hare:

To Roast a Hare

Take your hare when it is cased [skinned], and make a pudding [i.e. stuffing]:

Take a quarter of a pound of suet, and as much crumbs of bread, a little parsley shred fine, and about as much thyme as will lie on a sixpence, when shred; an anchovy shred small, a very little pepper and salt, some nutmeg, two eggs, and a little lemon-peel. Mix all these together, and put it into the hare.

Sew up the belly, spit it, and lay it to the fire, which must be a good one.

Your dripping-pan must be very clean and nice. Put in two quarts of milk and half a pound of butter into the pan: keep basting it all the time it is roasting, with the butter and milk, till the whole is used, and your hare will be enough.

You may mix the liver in the pudding if you like it. You must first parboil it, and then chop it fine.

To accompany the hare, Mrs Glasse recommends a sauce made from gravy and either 'currant jelly warmed in a cup', or 'red wine and sugar boiled to a syrup'.

1748

The Champion of the Potato The Parlement in France passed a law forbidding the cultivation of potatoes, on the grounds that they caused leprosy, among other ailments

– a suspicion perhaps based on the fact that the potato plant is related to deadly nightshade (as is the tomato and the tobacco plant). Potatoes had hitherto only been used for animal feed in France, although by 1755 *pommes frites* were being served at the banquets of the wealthy (*see* below).

But it was the French pharmacist and nutritionist Antoine-Auguste Parmentier (1737–1813) who really achieved the widespread acceptance in France of the potato as food for humans. While serving in the French army during the Seven Years War (1756–63), Parmentier was captured by the Prussians; during his imprisonment, he was obliged to survive on potatoes – and became a convert. Thanks to his efforts, in 1772 the Faculty of Medicine at the University of Paris declared potatoes fit for human consumption.

Parmentier continued to promote the benefits of the potato, hosting lavish dinner parties, with guests such as Benjamin Franklin and Antoine Lavoisier, at which a range of exotic potato dishes were served. Parmentier also presented the king and queen with bouquets of potato flowers, and placed an armed guard around his potato patch at Sablons, near Neuilly, west of Paris, to give the impression that his crop was of rare value. This had the desired effect: the local populace duly sneaked into the patch to filch the tubers, the armed guards having been instructed by Parmentier to accept all bribes, and to stand down at night. However, it was not until the bad harvests of 1785 that the potato gained wider acceptance in France. In his honour, many dishes involving potatoes have been named after Parmentier, including *hachis parmentier*, the French version of shepherd's (or cottage) pie.

circa 1750

The Tower of Plenty At Carnival time in the 18th century, the Bourbon kings of Naples would court the loyalty of their poorer subjects by erecting a *Cuccagna* – the Italian word for Cockaigne, the land of plenty. The Neapolitan *Cuccagna* was a multi-storey wooden tower built to represent a mountain, decked with green branches and artificial flowers. The tower contained masses of food and drink, together with live lambs and calves, while geese and pigeons were nailed by their wings to the walls. According to a contemporary eyewitness, when the king gave the signal, 'the mob fall on, destroy the building, carry off whatever they can lay hold of, and fight with each other till generally some fatal accident ensues'. The better-off found it all highly amusing. The tradition was abolished in 1779.

1755

From Pommes Frites to Freedom Fries The French cookery writer Menon (he is always known simply by that name) published *Les Soupers de la Cour* ('The Dinners of the Court'), which concerns itself with dining on a grand scale, from royal banquets to more modest dinner parties for 30 or 40 guests. More than a hundred dishes might be served at such dinner parties, in five courses, and among the recipes included is one for *pommes frites* ('fried potatoes'). The fact that a large quantity of oil was required to deep-fry the potatoes meant that at that time *pommes frites* were very much the preserve of the wealthy. It is thought that it was Thomas Jefferson who in the 1780s brought back the idea of *pommes frites* to the infant USA, and on the menu at a White House dinner in 1802 were 'potatoes served in the French manner'. Thereafter, in America the dish became known as 'French fried potatoes', then 'French fries', or just 'fries'. (In Britain, *pommes frites* are called 'chips', a term that in America and France denotes what the British call 'crisps'.) In reaction to the refusal of the French (xenophobically dubbed 'cheese-eating surrender monkeys') to join in the Iraq War in 2003, a temporary change of nomenclature was adopted in many US restaurants, whereby 'French fries' became 'freedom fries'. For a similar tale, involving French toast, *see* 1346.

Dr Johnson Insults Scottish National Dish In his *Dictionary of the English Language*, Samuel Johnson famously defined oats as 'A grain which in England is generally given to horses, but in Scotland supports the people.' The jibe was not forgotten. Following the 1773 visit of Dr Johnson to the University of St Andrews, where he was plied with French delicacies, the poet Robert Fergusson got in his retaliation, rousing his fellow Scots as follows:

But hear me lads! gin [if] I'd been there,
How I'd hae trimm'd the bill o' fare!
For ne'er sic [such] surly wight as he

Had met wi' sic respect frae me.
Mind ye what Sam, the lying loun [fellow]!
Has in his Dictionar laid down?
That aits in England are a feast
To cow an' horse, an' sican beast,
While in Scots ground this growth was common
To gust the gab [please the mouth] o' man and
   woman.

Fergusson then lists the Scottish dishes that he believes should have been served instead: haggis, sheep's head, and white and bloody puddings.

1756

Mahonnaise Sauce The French under the Duc de Richelieu took the port of Mahon, capital of the island of Minorca, from the British. (It was the failure of Admiral Byng to prevent this outcome that led to him being court-martialled and shot – '*pour encourager les autres*', as Voltaire famously quipped.) To celebrate his success, Richelieu ordered his chef to prepare a lavish banquet, but the chef, unable to lay his hands on any cream to prepare a typically rich French sauce, was obliged to improvise. Noting that the local aïoli – an emulsion of lemon juice and olive oil, stabilized with egg yolk and flavoured with raw garlic – was of a similar consistency to cream, he adapted it to his needs by omitting the garlic. The result was a great success with Richelieu, who dubbed the new sauce 'Mahonnaise' to commemorate his victory. Later, this name evolved into the familiar word we use today: mayonnaise.

1757

Tea: the Root of All Misery In his *Essay on Tea*, Jonas Hanway lamented the deleterious effect of the beverage: 'Men seem to have lost their stature, and comeliness; and women their beauty. Your very chambermaids have lost their bloom, I suppose by sipping tea.' The 'execrable custom' of tea drinking, Hanway contended, diverted servants and other manual workers from honest labour, and also meant that for poor people there was less money for bread. Thus he describes how he found in the poorest dwellings 'men and women sipping their tea, in the morning or afternoon, and very often both morning and afternoon: those will have tea who have not bread . . . misery itself had no power to banish tea, which had frequently introduced that misery.' Tea resulted in the 'bad nursing of children', and, what was worse, 'this flatulent liquor shortens the lives of great numbers of people'. Indeed, he concludes that, 'since tea has been in fashion, even *suicide* has been more familiar amongst us than in times past'.

In 1821 William Cobbett, in *The Vice of Tea-Drinking*, took up Hanway's theme, regretting that tea was taking the place of good old ale:

It is notorious that tea has no useful strength in it; and that it contains nothing nutritious; that it, besides being good for nothing, has badness in it, because it is well-known to produce want of sleep in many cases, and in all cases, to shake and weaken the nerves.

To put it in a nutshell:

I view the tea drinking as a destroyer of health, an enfeebler of the frame, an engenderer of effeminacy and laziness, a debaucher of youth, and a maker of misery for old age.

A Trifling Thing

In 1759 the English cook William Verral, who had worked for the Duke of Newcastle before taking over the White Hart Inn in Lewes, published *A Complete System of Cookery*, a lively work which reflected his apprenticeship under the renowned French chef, Monsieur de Saint-Clouet. Here is one of his simpler recipes:

Anchovies, with Parmesan Cheese

Fry some bits of bread about the length of an anchovy in good oil or butter.

Lay the half of an anchovy, with the bone upon each bit, and strew over them some Parmesan cheese grated fine, and colour them nicely in an oven, or with a salamander [a circular iron plate, heated and placed over a dish to brown it].

Squeeze the juice of an orange or lemon, and pile them up in your dish and send them to the table.

This seems to be but a trifling thing, but I never saw it come whole from the table.

At the time of the publication of Verral's work, Britain was embroiled in the Seven Years War with France, and Verral's adherence to the French style of cookery was regarded as deeply suspect by the more jingoistic of his readers. A contributor to the *Critical Review* (Volume 8, 1759), for one, could barely contain himself:

It is entitled *A Complete System of Cookery*; but, what if it should prove *A Complete System of Politics*, aye, and of damnable politics, considering the present critical situation of affairs! If not a system of politics, at least, it may be supposed to be a political system trumped up in favour of our inveterate enemies the French. Nay, the author forgets himself so far as even to own, in the preface, that his chief end is to show the whole and simple art of the most modern and best French cookery. Ah, ha! Master William Verral, have we caught you tripping? We wish there may not be some Jesuitical ingredients in this French cookery . . . [etcetera, etcetera]

1759

A Love of Music and Food Part One: Handel Eats for Two The German-British composer George Frideric Handel died on 14 April. Handel appears to have been something of a trencherman, if one is to believe the story told by the 18th-century music historian Charles Burney. One evening Handel ordered dinner for two from a local tavern, and asked his landlord to send it up when it arrived. The landlord asked if he was expecting company, to which Handel replied, 'I am the company.'

1762

Who Invented the Sandwich? John Montagu, 4th Earl of Sandwich, the politician and patron of the arts, was so reluctant to leave the card table to dine that he had his servant put a piece of cold beef between two slices of bread – so creating what became known as the sandwich. So goes the commonly told story, but by the standards of the day Sandwich was not such an inveterate gambler, and indeed his biographer N.A.M. Rodger suggests that, busy man of affairs that he was, Sandwich may well have ordered the first sandwich so that he could eat at his desk.

Sandwich's sandwich was not, in fact, the first sandwich. Fourteen years earlier, the famous courtesan Fanny Murray – one of whose most regular clients was Sandwich himself – was so disdainful of the £20 note presented to her by Sir Richard Atkins for her top-of-the-range services that she 'clapped' the note between two pieces of bread and butter and ate it. (Incidentally, Lord Chancellor Hardwicke claimed to have seen, in the collection of Sandwich's brother, William Montague, a joint portrait of Fanny Murray and another famous courtesan, Kitty Fisher, both of them naked.)

1764

Rosemary and the Dead In his *Dictionnaire raisonné universel d'histoire naturelle*, the French naturalist Jacques-Christophe Valmont de Bomare recounted how, when coffins were opened after a number of years, the sprigs of rosemary that had been placed in the hands of the deceased had grown and flourished, covering the corpse. He does not inform us whether rosemary cultivated in such circumstances has any distinctive culinary qualities.

circa 1765

The First Restaurant The French word *restaurant* (which literally means 'restoring') had been applied since the 15th century to any food, cordial or medicine thought to restore health and vigour – specifically a fortifying meat broth. However, it was not used of an establishment serving food until a certain Monsieur Boulanger, a seller of this broth, put up a sign outside his premises in Paris with the dog Latin slogan, *Venite ad me, vos qui stomacho laboratis, et ego restaurabo vos* ('Come to me, you with labouring stomachs, and I will restore you').

1769

Infested Biscuits In September, Joseph Banks, chief naturalist on Captain Cook's first voyage to the South Seas, commented in his journal on the 'quantity of Vermin' (i.e. weevils) that were to be found in ship's biscuit, also known as hardtack, the staple food of the mariner of the period:

> I have often seen hundreds, nay thousands shaken out of a single biscuit. We in the [officers'] cabin had however an easy remedy for this by baking it in an oven, not too hot, which makes them all walk off.

Banks described the taste of the weevils as 'strong as mustard or rather spirits of hartshorn'.

Hardtack – also a staple for troops during land campaigns of the time – was basic fare, comprising flour and water mixed into a paste and baked twice. Salt might be added in the more luxurious versions. Alternative names included dog biscuits, tooth-dullers, molar-breakers, sheet iron and worm castles. For long voyages, it was baked four times, six months prior to departure, and, as long as it remained dry, it kept indefinitely – unless entirely consumed by weevils. During the American Civil War, the soldiers would dunk their biscuit in coffee to soften it, with the added bonus that the weevil larvae would float to the top, where they could be skimmed off.

The Fattest Hog in Epicurus' Sty The eminent Scottish philosopher David Hume was also a passionate devotee of the culinary art, a weakness to which he openly confessed in a letter to Sir Gilbert Elliot dated October 1769:

> Cookery, the Science to which I intend to addict the remaining years of my Life . . . for Beef and Cabbage (a charming dish) and old Mutton, old Claret, no body excels me.

Hume's figure and his fondness for food led William Mason to describe him, in 'An Heroic Epistle to Sir William Chambers', as 'the fattest hog in Epicurus' sty'. Meanwhile Lord Charlemont, who had met Hume in Italy in 1748, described the great philosopher as resembling 'a turtle-eating alderman'.

To Make a Pease Soup for Lent

In 1769 Elizabeth Raffald, formerly housekeeper to Sir Peter and Lady Elizabeth Warburton, published *The Experienced English Housekeeper*, 'consisting of near 800 original receipts, most of which never appeared in print'. Here is her recipe for a Lenten pea soup:

Put three pints of blue boiling peas into five quarts of soft cold water, three anchovies, three red herrings, and two large onions, stick in a clove at each end, a carrot and a parsnip sliced in, with a bunch of sweet herbs.

Boil them all together 'till the soup is thick.

Strain it through a colander, then slice in the white part of a head of celery, a good lump of butter, a little pepper and salt, a slice of bread toasted and butter'd well, and cut in little diamonds, put it into the dish, and pour the soup upon it; and a little dried mint if you choose it.

So successful was her book that Mrs Raffald was able to sell the copyright for the then substantial sum of £1400.

1771

London Bread: A Deleterious Paste In his novel *The Expedition of Humphy Clinker*, Tobias Smollett has one of his characters complain:

The bread I eat in London is a deleterious paste, mixed up with chalk, alum and bone ashes, insipid to the taste and destructive to the constitution. The good people are not ignorant of this adulteration; but they prefer it to wholesome bread, because it is whiter than the meal of corn [wheat]. Thus they sacrifice their taste and their health . . . to a most absurd gratification of a misjudged eye; and the miller or the baker is obliged to poison them and their families, in order to live by his profession.

French Food Part One: A Parcel of Kickshaws In the same novel, Smollett decried French food as not only unwholesome, but unmanly:

As to the repast, it was made up of a parcel of kickshaws, contrived by a French cook, without one substantial article adapted to the satisfaction of an English appetite. The pottage was little better than bread soaked in dish washings, luke-warm. The ragouts looked as if they had been once eaten and half digested: the fricassees were involved in a nasty yellow poultice; and the rotis were scorched and stinking, for the honour of the fumet. The dessert consisted of faded fruit and iced froth, a good emblem of our landlady's character; the table-beer was sour, the water foul, and the wine vapid.

The Admirable Thompson Captain Cook returned from his first voyage to the Southern Ocean, having embarked three years previously. Many demands were made during the expedition upon the ingenuity of the cook, John Thompson, who had to come up with recipes for such unusual items as dog, cormorant and penguin. Cook described the flesh of the latter as 'reminiscent of bullock's liver'. (Incidentally, for his last Christmas dinner before his fatal journey to the South Pole, Captain Scott also enjoyed penguin: 'an entrée of stewed penguin's breasts and red currant jelly – the dish fit for an epicure and not unlike jugged hare'.)

As for Thompson's recipe for albatross, the expedition naturalist, Joseph Banks, gave this account:

> The way of dressing them is thus: skin them over-night and soak their carcases in salt water till morn, then parboil them and throw away the water, then stew them well with very little water and when sufficiently tender serve them up with a savoury sauce.

The result was apparently so good 'that everybody commended them and ate heartily of them, [as] though there was fresh pork upon the table'.

1773

On the Uselessness of Cucumbers On 5 October, Dr Johnson pronounced: 'It has been a common saying of physicians in England, that a cucumber should be well sliced, and dressed with pepper and vinegar, and then thrown out, as good for nothing.' Not everybody shared this opinion, as attested by this anonymous rhyme from the 19th century:

> I love my little cucumber
> So long, so firm, so straight.
> So sad, my little cucumber,
> We cannot propagate.

1775

The Perils of the Grand Tour While travelling in Italy, Lady Miller was horrified at what she was served for supper in a village near Ferrara:

A pork soup with the bouillée in it, namely a hog's head with the eyelashes, eyes and nose on, the very food the wretched animal had last eaten of before he made his exit remained sticking about the teeth.

The soup, having been removed untasted, was replaced by a dish of boiled house sparrows. 'Need I say,' her ladyship concludes, 'we went to bed supperless.' She was not the only English person on the Grand Tour who was appalled by Italian country fare. Others complained of being faced with 'mustard and crow's gizzards' or 'an egg, a frog and bad wine', while one unfortunate was obliged to drink wine mixed with water in which there were a multitude of tadpoles – a circumstance addressed with pluck and ingenuity: 'While I held the pitcher to my lips, I formed a dam with a knife, to prevent the little frogs from slipping down my throat.'

1779

Royal Table Manners In his *Reminiscences* (1826) the celebrated Irish tenor Michael Kelly recalled his time in Naples in 1779, where he studied at the Conservatorio Santa Maria di Loreto. While in the city he became the protégé of Sir William Hamilton, the British ambassador, who arranged for him to be presented to King Ferdinand IV, for whom he sang. When the party sat down to dine, Kelly was astonished at the way the king set about a bowl of pasta:

He seized it in his fingers, twisting and pulling it about, and cramming it voraciously into his mouth, most magnanimously disdaining the use of either knife, fork or spoon, or indeed any aid except such as nature had kindly afforded him.

Ferdinand had something of a reputation for boorishness, kicking the bottoms of his courtiers, groping his queen (the sister of Marie Antoinette) in public, and on one occasion scuttling after his fleeing retainers with his breeches round his ankles demanding that they inspect the contents of the chamber pot he brandished in his hands.

circa 1780

Painful Puns Dr Johnson's biographer James Boswell, together with two of his cronies, indulged in some shocking wordplay while taking tea – as here recounted by the novelist and raconteur Henry Mackenzie (1745–1831):

Lord Kelly, a determined punster, and his brother Andrew were drinking tea with James Boswell. Boswell put his cup to his head, 'Here's *t'ye*, my Lord.' – At that moment, Lord Kelly coughed. – 'You have a *coughie*,' said his brother. – 'Yes,' said Lord Kelly, 'I have been like to *choak o' late*.'

1781

Tripping on Raw Pork Henry Fuseli painted *The Nightmare*, a phantasmagoria that encapsulates the dark side of the Romantic imagination. In conceiving of his subject, it was rumoured that Fuseli drew on the dreams he experienced after eating raw pork chops – a practice traditionally believed to induce visions. Lord Byron alluded to this belief when he dismissed the poetry of Keats as nothing but 'a Bedlam vision produced by raw pork and opium'.

The Strange Consequence of Eating Asparagus Benjamin Franklin penned a cod letter 'To the Royal Academy of Farting', in which he proffered a specific against a well-known side-effect of eating asparagus:

> A few stems of asparagus eaten, shall give our urine a disagreeable odour; and a pill of turpentine no bigger than a pea, shall bestow on it the pleasing smell of violets.

Similar advice is given in that bible of Italian cookery, Pellegrino Artusi's *Science in the Kitchen and the Art of Eating Well* (1891), which suggests one puts a few drops of turpentine in one's chamber pot. About 50 per cent of people find that eating asparagus lends their urine an unusual smell. This effect is the result of the metabolizing of the asparagusic acid in the vegetable into various sulphur-containing compounds.

1782

The United Salad of America By Act of Congress, the phrase *E pluribus unum* (Latin for 'out of many, one') was adopted as one of the mottos on the seal of the infant USA. The phrase derives from one used in '*Moretum*', a Latin poem attributed to Virgil (70–19 BC):

> *It manus in gyrum; paullatim singula vires*
> *Deperdunt proprias; color est e pluribus unus.*

In John Augustine Wilstach's 1884 verse translation, this is rendered as:

> Spins round the stirring hand; lose by degrees
> Their separate powers the parts, and comes at last
> From many several colours one that rules.

Moretum means 'garden herbs', and the poem describes the making of a salad of garlic, parsley, rue and onions, seasoned with cheese, salt, coriander and vinegar, and finally sprinkled with oil.

Toast 'Incomparable' In his *Journeys of a German in England in the Year 1782* (published the following year) the German author Karl Philipp Moritz waxed lyrical about one aspect of English food:

> The slices of bread and butter given to you with tea are as thin as poppy-leaves, but there is a way of roasting slices of buttered bread before the fire which is incomparable. One slice after another is taken and held to the fire with a fork until the butter is melted, then the following one will be always laid upon it so that the butter soaks through the whole pile of slices. This is called 'toast'.

The idea of toast as a way of making stale bread more palatable was not in fact an English innovation, but originated with the Romans, and the word itself comes from Latin *tostare*, meaning 'to parch'. The other sort of toast, in which one raises a glass to someone, has the same origin. When the word first entered the English language in the 15th century, it denoted a piece of bread browned at the fire and put into wine or ale (perhaps to improve the flavour) – as when Falstaff demands in *The Merry Wives of Windsor* (III.v) 'Go fetch me a quart of sack; put a toast in't.' The word 'toast' in the sense of a lady to whom the company raises its glass results from a figurative transference: the name of the lady supposedly flavoured one's glass in the same way as did a piece of spiced toast.

> Then, said he, Why do you call live people toasts?
> I answered, That was a new name found out by the
> wits to make a lady have the same effect as burridge
> [borage] in the glass when a man is drinking.
>
> Richard Steele, in *The Tatler*, No. 31 (1709)

1784

A Hot Potato Dr Samuel Johnson died. There is a possibly apocryphal story that once while dining Johnson spat out a hot potato, to the alarm of the assembled company. Johnson turned to his shocked hostess and explained, 'Madam, a fool would have swallowed that.'

Johnson took his food seriously, as Boswell recorded in his *Life* of the great man:

> Some people have a foolish way of not minding, or
> pretending not to mind, what they eat. For my part,
> I mind my belly very studiously and very carefully;
> for I look upon it that he who does not mind his
> belly will hardly mind anything else.

On another occasion Johnson boasted: 'I could write a better book about cookery than has ever been written.' He never did, though.

The Café of the Blind The Palais Royal in Paris was reopened after refurbishment as a complex of shops, cafés, bars, sideshows and other forms of entertainment. One of its more notorious establishments was the Café des Aveugles ('Café of the Blind'), which had a score of private rooms where customers could indulge in all kinds of debauched behaviour, without worrying what the café's musicians might see – because the members of the café's small orchestra were all blind.

In 1805 the complex was enlivened by the addition of Le Caveau du Sauvage ('The Cellar of the Savage'), opened by a man who had formerly been Robespierre's coachman, and where for the price of two sols clients could watch 'copulating savages'. Another of the must-go destinations in the Palais Royal was the Café Mécanique, where orders were given to the kitchen by means of a speaking tube, and food was delivered to diners on a plate that rose from below into the middle of each table.

1785

The Wrong Scotch In Captain Grose's *Classical Dictionary of the Vulgar Tongue* we find a fearsome drink called

'Scotch chocolate', which, according to the author, consists of 'brimstone and milk'. Several decades later, in the Victorian era, sailors would drink something called 'Scotch coffee', comprising hot water flavoured with burnt biscuit. In both instances, the allusion appears to be to the proverbial meanness of the Scots. An even more invidious concoction associated with the Scots in the following century was the so-called 'stair-heid shandy' once drunk in the tenement slums of Glasgow; this consisted of a pint of milk through which coal gas had been passed, for the narcotic effect.

1787

Towards a Sublime Concentration The French nobleman, Charles, Prince de Soubise, died. He had employed a chef who believed in only the finest and most concentrated of stocks as the basis of his sauces, and to this end had once asked the prince for fifty hams.

'Fifty hams, sir? Why, you will ruin me!' expostulated the prince.

'Ah, Monsieur,' replied the chef, 'but give me those hams and I will reduce them into a phial the size of my thumb, and make with it something wonderful!'

The chef had his way.

Address to a Haggis Robert Burns published his famous poem in praise of the Scottish national dish:

> Fair fa' your honest, sonsie [ruddy] face,
> Great chieftain o' the puddin-race!

In fact haggis – which comprises minced sheep offal, oatmeal, suet, seasonings and finely chopped onion, wrapped in a sheep's stomach lining and boiled – is not exclusively Scottish. Until 1700 or thereabouts it was eaten in England; what is more, the earliest known recipe appears in a 15th-century manuscript from Lancashire, and the earliest printed recipe is in Gervase Markham's *The English Huswife* (1615). The classic recipe, however, is that supplied by Meg Dods in 1826 (*see* page 204). More modern recipes involving haggis include 'Flying Scotsman' (chicken breast stuffed with haggis) and 'Chicken Balmoral' (like Flying Scotsman, but with a bacon wrapping). Haggis bhaji is on the menu of certain Indian restaurants in Glasgow, while in Edinburgh one can buy haggis-flavoured chocolate truffles. The importation of haggis into the USA was banned from 1989 to 2010, for fear that it might carry scrapie, the sheep version of mad cow disease.

Little Worms In a letter dated 27 November to Lady Hesketh, the poet William Cowper recounted the following incident:

> A poor man begged food at the Hall lately. The cook gave him some vermicelli soup. He ladled it about some time with the spoon, and then returned it to her, saying, 'I am but a poor man, it is true, and I am very hungry, but yet I cannot eat broth with maggots in it.'

The poor man had a point: the Italian word *vermicelli*, the thin, string-like pasta used in soups, literally means 'little worms'.

The Stomach of Ostriches In his journal while travelling in Spain and Portugal, William Beckford had this to say:

> The Portuguese had need have the stomach of ostriches to digest the loads of greasy victuals with which they cram themselves. Their vegetables, their rice, their poultry are all stewed in the essence of ham and so strongly seasoned with pepper and spices that a spoonful of pease or a quarter of onion is sufficient to set one's mouth in a flame. With such a

diet and the continual swallowing of sweetmeats, I am not surprised at their complaining continually of headaches and vapours.

1788

The Monster Pies of Denby Dale The White Hart Inn in Denby Dale in Yorkshire baked a massive game pie to celebrate the fact that King George III had recovered his sanity (only temporarily, as it turned out). The pie, a sort of 'stand pie', in which the crust supports the pie without the need of a dish, was served to the villagers in the field behind the pub.

Since then, the villagers have baked several more gargantuan pies to mark various occasions of particular moment.

The 1815 pie celebrated Wellington's victory at Waterloo. The celebrations were attended by George Wilby, a veteran of the battle and a native of the village. The pie was baked at the Corn Mill, and probably included several chickens and a couple of sheep. Wilby was given the honour of cutting the pie with his sword.

The 1846 pie celebrated the repeal of the Corn Laws, which, by preventing the import of cheap foreign grain, kept the price of bread high, leading to widespread hardship in the 'Hungry Forties'. The 1846 pie was 7 feet 10 inches in diameter, nearly 2 feet deep, and contained 100 pounds of beef, 1 calf, 5 sheep, 21 rabbits and hares, and 89 assorted game birds and poultry. It took ten and a half hours to bake, and was so heavy that the stage on which it was placed to be cut up collapsed. The crowd of 15,000, frantic with hunger, then rushed forward to grab what they could, with the result that the pie was trampled underfoot. Some say the collapse of the stage was engineered by pro-Corn Law Tories, or by the rival village of Clayton West (which had just baked a giant plum pie), or that the speechifying was so tedious that two local lads, determined to spice up proceedings, knocked down the supports of the stage – with the result that the speechifier, a certain Mr Hinchcliffe, was tipped into the pie.

The 1887 pie celebrated Queen Victoria's Golden Jubilee. In order to avoid the fiasco of 1846, an organizing committee arranged for the pie dish to be built out of iron and steel by a Huddersfield firm more used to constructing gasometers. A special oven was constructed behind the White Hart Inn, adjacent to a giant stewing boiler to cook the meat: 1581 pounds of beef, 163 pounds of veal, 180 pounds of lamb, 180 pounds of mutton, 250 pounds of pork, 67 rabbits and hares, and 153 game birds and poultry – not to mention 588 pounds of potatoes. The meat was cooked in batches in the boiler, being added bit by bit to the pie – a very slow process – while the game birds were added raw, with the idea that they would cook in the oven. The result was, that when the pie was eventually cut open before another enormous crowd, the air filled with the nauseating stench of rotting meat. The next day the pie was dragged to Toby Wood, buried in quicklime and mourned with the following verse:

Tho' lost to sight, yet still to memory dear,
We smell it yet as tho' it still was here;
Tho' short its life and quick was its decay,
We thought it best to bury it without the least delay.

To restore the honour of the village, the ladies of Denby Dale promptly set to work to make a replacement 'Resurrection Pie', containing 1 heifer, 2 calves, 2 sheep, 1344 pounds of potatoes – and no game birds.

The 1896 pie marked the 50th anniversary of the repeal of the Corn Laws. The pie again eschewed game birds, and before it was served it was certified as fit for consumption by a medical officer of health. In addition, the stage was specially reinforced, and railings erected to prevent a crowd surge.

The 1928 pie was belatedly baked to commemorate victory in the Great War. This time the villagers deliberately set out to bake the world's biggest ever pie. It was rectangular in shape, measuring 16 by 5 feet, and 15 inches deep;

it contained 4 bullocks and 15 hundredweight of potatoes, and took 30 hours to cook. The only hitch was that the dish got stuck in the oven, and was only freed by knocking part of the wall down.

The 1964 pie celebrated four royal births (Prince Edward, Lady Helen Windsor, Lady Sarah Armstrong Jones and James Ogilvy). The pie was even bigger – 18 by 6 feet, and 18 inches deep, weighing 6.5 tons – and its recipe was advised upon by a panel of experts, including Clement Freud. A total of 30,000 servings were sold and eaten within one hour.

The 1988 pie marked the bicentenary of the first pie. This was another record pie: 20 by 7 feet, and 18 inches deep, and its contents were measured metrically – 3000 kilograms of beef, the same again of potatoes, and 750 kilograms of onions. Environmental health legislation required that a method be found of keeping the pie sufficiently hot while it was paraded around the village prior to consumption, and this was achieved by means of hot water piped around the dish. Some 100,000 visitors arrived on Pie Day, and £8000 was raised to purchase Wither Wood, now managed by the Woodland Trust.

The 2000 pie was the Millennium Pie. The 12-tonne monster again broke all records, measuring 40 by 8 feet, and 44 inches deep. The project involved a Rotherham sheet-metal company and the School of Engineering at the

University of Huddersfield. In addition to the usual gargantuan quantities of beef, potatoes and onions, the pie also contained gallons of beer, and was blessed by the Bishop of Wakefield.

1789

Another Debt to Jefferson Thomas Jefferson, then American minister plenipotentiary in Paris, asked a young friend visiting Naples to bring him back a macaroni machine. The young friend duly obliged, and the machine became the first of its kind in the USA when Jefferson returned home in September of the same year. It is unknown whether Jefferson followed the advice of the Parisian pasta-maker Paul-Jacques Malouin, who in 1767 had advised that the best lubricant for a pasta machine is a little oil mixed with boiled cow brains.

1790

Nothing so Dainty as Elephant Foot In his *Travels from the Cape of Good Hope into the Interior Parts of Africa*, François LeVaillant recounts how he breakfasted with a group of Hottentots upon baked elephant's foot, leaving us the following encomium:

It exhaled such a savoury odour, that I soon tasted it and found it to be delicious. I had often heard the feet of bears commended, but could not conceive that so gross and heavy an animal as the elephant would afford such delicate food. 'Never,' said I, 'can our modern epicures have such a dainty at their tables; let forced fruits and the contributions of various countries contribute to their luxury, yet cannot they procure so excellent a dish as I have now before me.

In contrast, two centuries later Laurens van der Post, in *First Catch Your Eland: A Taste of Africa* (1977), states that elephant flesh has 'too giant a texture ever to be truly palatable'. Nevertheless, he records that in certain parts of the continent, British district commissioners would always eat a dish of elephant head and trotters on Sundays. Giraffe, on the other hand, he avers is 'perhaps the oldest and most sought after delicacy of primitive man in Africa'. Regarding the giraffe, C. Louis Leipoldt, in *Leipoldt's Cape Cookery* (1976), adds that 'the long succulent tongue, properly cooked, is not only eatable but delectable'. However, it should be pointed out that the giraffe is protected throughout most of its range. Leipoldt also recommends lion meat (apparently comparable to venison), especially lion steaks marinated in wine and vinegar, and then fried.

1794

A Miser's Diet Daniel Dancer, the notorious miser, died on 30 September. Although worth £3000 per annum, Dancer would dress himself largely in bundles of hay. He did splash out on a new shirt once a year – and once went to law with his shirt-supplier over one such transaction, claiming he had been cheated out of threepence. Dancer ate but one meal a day, consisting of a little baked meat and a hard-boiled dumpling. His only friend, Lady Tempest (to whom he left his fortune), once gave him a brace of trout, but, fearing the expense of lighting a fire, Dancer attempted to warm up the fish by sitting on them.

1799

British Food Part Two: Only One Sauce The Neapolitan diplomat Francesco Caracciolo died. He once had famously observed that 'In England there are sixty different religions, and only one sauce.'

THE 19TH CENTURY

1800

Cognac vs Whisky The following story is told of a certain John Wilsone, who was president of Glasgow's Beefsteak Club at the turn of the 19th century, at a time when all good British reactionaries abhorred the democratic principles emanating from Revolutionary France:

At a meeting of the club, on a particular occasion, Mr Wilsone observed a member tossing off a glass of whisky, and following it up immediately by a bumper of brandy. The witty president at once exclaimed, 'Good God, sir! what are you about? You have disgraced yourself and the club, by putting a fiddling Frenchman above a sturdy Highlander.' The copper-nosed delinquent instantly started to his feet, swallowed another jorum of Ferintosh, and laying his hand upon his heart, said, 'Brand me not with being a democrat, sir; for now I've got the Frenchman between two fires!'

The 'Rambling Reporter', notes to the 1887 reprint
of *Jones's Directory for the Year 1787*

Chicken Marengo

On 14 June 1800 Napoleon Bonaparte won a decisive

victory near the little village of Marengo in Pied-mont, leading to the expulsion of the Austrians from Italy. After the battle, the famished Napoleon asked his chef Durand to prepare him something to eat. A quick forage produced a handful of ingredients, and Durand came up with the following recipe:

Take one scrawny farmyard chicken, cut it up with a sabre, and fry it in olive oil (in the absence of butter) until browned on all sides.

Add some garlic, roughly chopped tomatoes and some water, and place a crayfish on top to steam.

Allow the ingredients to simmer until the meat is tender.

Add a dash of cognac from Napoleon's own flask.

Serve with fried eggs and lashings of fried army-issue bread, the staler the better.

Napoleon was delighted with the result, and was to order his chef to prepare what became known as 'chicken Marengo' again and again.

That at least is the story, although some authori-ties suggest that the recipe was actually invented in a Paris restaurant several years after the battle. In addition, some food historians doubt that tomatoes would have been readily available in northern Italy at that time. Today, chicken Marengo usually also includes some dry white wine, mushrooms and parsley, while the crayfish, cognac and eggs are generally omitted.

1808

Teaching the French How to Eat Prince Alexander Borisovich Kurakin, known as the 'Diamond Prince' owing to the magnificence of his costumes, became Russia's ambassador in Paris. It was Kurakin who is credited with introducing to France *service à la russe* – 'service in the Russian style' – in which at a grand dinner the courses are brought to the table one by one. This is as opposed to *service à la française*, the ostentatious style then prevalent in France, in which all the courses are placed on the table at the same time, and the guests help themselves.

The Health Benefits of Red Wine The English lawyer William Hickey began to write his celebrated *Memoirs* (not published until a century later). Among many other things, Hickey recalls how Sir John Royds, a judge in the service of the East India Company, was 'indebted to claret for his very unexpected recovery; during the last week of the disease they poured down his throat from three to four bottles of that generous beverage every four-and-twenty hours, and with extraordinary effect.'

1810

The First Curry House The Indian surgeon, traveller and entrepreneur Sake Dean Mahomed opened the first curry house in England, namely the Hindoostanee Coffee House in George Street, London. Here Dean Mahomed offered to old East India Company hands dishes 'allowed by the greatest epicures to be unequalled to any'. Despite the availability of 'Indian dishes in the highest perfection', the restaurant closed within a year, and in 1814 Dean Mahomed moved to Brighton with his Irish wife Jane. Here he opened a health establishment, 'the Indian Medicated Vapour Bath (type of Turkish bath), a cure to many diseases and giving full relief when everything fails; particularly rheumatic and paralytic, gout, stiff joints, old sprains, lame legs, aches and pains in the joints'. His new establishment, which involved two novelties, namely shampoo and massage, was a huge success, and its proprietor became known as 'Dr Brighton'.

The oldest surviving curry house in the UK is Veeraswamy in London's Regent Street, which opened in 1926. Its first proprietor was Edward Palmer, the great-grandson of an English soldier and an Indian princess. Its clientele has included Winston Churchill, King Gustav VI of Sweden, Jawaharlal Nehru, Indira Gandhi and Charlie Chaplin.

1811

The Comet Vintages The Flaugergues Comet, also known as the Great Comet of 1811, made its appearance, marking the first of the so-called 'comet vintages' – years in which the appearance of a comet has coincided with a wine vintage of exceptional quality. Other comet vintages include 1826, 1839, 1845, 1852, 1858, 1861, 1985 and 1989 – although sceptics point out that there have been plenty of fine vintages in non-comet years. It might also be pointed out that although the appearance of Halley's Comet towards the end of 1985 coincided with a remarkable vintage, its 1910 appearance did not – in Champagne, for example, nearly the entire crop was lost to hailstorms and floods.

In 1811, the most celebrated of the comet vintages, the comet in question was first spotted by Honoré de Flaugergues in March, and it was visible through much of the growing season, which was characterized by perfect conditions – particularly welcome after the succession of poor vintages that had marked the early years of the century. In Champagne, 1811 saw the development by the house of Veuve Cliquot of the modern *méthode champenoise*, by which sediments were removed while preserving the carbon dioxide responsible for the bubbles. The 1811 vintage port was also exceptional, as recorded by George Borrow in *The Romany Rye* (1857):

He then rang the bell, and having ordered two fresh glasses to be brought, he went out and presently returned with a small pint bottle, which he uncorked with his own hand; then sitting down he said, 'The wine that I bring here is port of eighteen hundred and eleven, the year of the comet, the best vintage on record. The wine which we have been drinking,' he added, 'is good, but not to be compared with this, which I never sell, and I am chary of. When you have drunk some of it, I think you will own that I have conferred an obligation upon you.' He then filled the glasses, the wine which he poured out diffusing an aroma through the room . . .

But the most celebrated wines of the 1811 vintage are the Bordeaux whites of Château d'Yquem, which were given the ultimate '100 points' in a 1996 tasting by wine guru Robert Parker. Although most white wines go off within a few years, Château d'Yquem is a noted exception, owing to the preservative properties of the natural acidity of the grapes combined with the high levels of residual sugar. On 26 July 2011 a bottle of 1811 Château d'Yquem sold for £75,000 at auction in London – the highest price ever paid for a bottle of white wine.

A Herculean Tippler The Irish politician Sir Hercules Langrishe, a noted toper, died. One evening, a friend, astonished that he had apparently managed to finish off three bottles of port at a single sitting, asked him whether he had had any assistance. 'None,' replied Sir Hercules, 'save that of a bottle of Madeira.'

1814

A Demand for Fast Food Austrian, Prussian and Russian forces occupied Paris, obliging Napoleon's first abdication and his temporary exile to Elba. Such was the clamour of the hungry Allied soldiers to be served at the eating establishments of Paris that the Russian cry of '*Bystro*' ('quickly') could often be heard in the streets. There is a story that this gave rise to the French word *bistro*, denoting a modest restaurant – although sceptics point out that the word *bistro* is not recorded until the late 19th century. Another theory contends that the word derives from *bistrouille*, a liqueur coffee.

1817

The Voluptuous Madame Véry Stamford Raffles, the founder of Singapore, visited the highly fashionable Véry's restaurant in the Palais Royal, Paris, and was struck by Madame Véry herself:

> On entering the room, the first object that arrested the attention was the mistress, a young and beautiful woman, most elegantly dressed, reclining at her ease on an elevated seat. Around her the waiters gather to receive her orders and to make reports of the progress of affairs.

It was said that Monsieur and Madame Véry only received permission to open up in the desirable Palais Royal after the latter had promised the minister of the interior that 'she would favour him with her company to supper and not forget to put her nightcap in her pocket'.

Véry's was the setting for a famous story in which a Prussian general, after the defeat of Napoleon, ordered coffee in a cup 'from which no Frenchman had drunk'. The waiter brought him his coffee in a chamber pot.

1818

Shelley in Garlic Shock Writing from Naples on 22 December, the English poet Percy Bysshe Shelley could not make up his mind about Italy:

> There are *two* Italies . . . The one is the most sublime and lovely contemplation that can be conceived by the imagination of man; the other is the most degraded, disgusting, and odious. What do you think? Young women of rank actually eat – you will never guess what – *garlick*!

A century or so later, Shelley's compatriot Hilaire Belloc also expressed an aversion to certain aspects of Italian cuisine:

In Italy, the traveller notes
With great disgust the flesh of goats
Appearing on the table d'hotes;
And even this the natives spoil
By frying it in rancid oil.

1819

In Praise of Claret In a letter dated 18 February to his brother and sister-in-law George and Georgina, the poet John Keats wrote the following encomium:

I like claret . . . For really 'tis so fine – it fills one's mouth with a gushing freshness – then you do not feel it quarrelling with your liver – no, it is rather a Peacemaker, and lies as quiet as it did in the grape; then it is as fragrant as the Queen Bee, and the more ethereal part of it mounts into the Brain, not assaulting the cerebral apartments like a bully in a badhouse looking for his trull, and hurrying from door to door bouncing against the wainscot, but rather walks like Aladdin about his enchanted place so gently that you do not feel his step.

1820

An Intimate Relationship On 20 November, the whaleship *Essex* was struck and sunk by a sperm whale – an incident that partly inspired Herman Melville's epic novel *Moby-Dick* (1851). The crew of the *Essex* found themselves adrift in small boats, and out of 21 men only 8 survived. Many years later one of the survivors, the ship's captain, George Pollard, was approached by a relative of one of the lost sailors, and was asked whether he remembered the man. 'Remember him?' roared Pollard. 'Hell, son, I et him.'

1823

A Dislike of Lard Heralds the Beginning of Decadence In his book *Cottage Economy*, William Cobbett – that upholder of the rural virtues – lamented the decline in the English taste for hog lard:

> Country children are badly brought up if they do not like sweet lard spread upon bread, as we spread butter. Many a score hunches [hunks of bread] of this sort have I eaten, and I never knew what poverty was. I have eaten it for luncheon at the houses of good substantial farmers in France and Flanders. I am not now frequently so hungry as I ought to be;

but I should think it no hardship to eat *sweet* lard instead of butter. But, now-a-days, the labourers, and especially the female part of them, have fallen into the taste of *niceness* in food and *finery in dress*; a quarter of a bellyful and rags are the consequence.

1825

Those Who Enjoy Their Food, and Those Who Do Not Two months before his death, the French gastronome Jean Anthelme Brillat-Savarin published *Physiologie du goût* ('Physiology of Taste'), in which he famously stated, 'Tell me what you eat, and I will tell you what you are', and 'The discovery of a new dish confers more happiness on humanity, than the discovery of a new star.' Brillat-Savarin has this to say on the kinds of people who make the best gastronomes:

Those predisposed to epicurism are for the most part of middling height. They are broad-faced and have bright eyes, small forehead, short nose, fleshy lips and rounded chin. The women are plump, chubby, pretty rather than beautiful, with a slight tendency to fullness of figure . . .

Those, on the contrary, to whom nature has denied an aptitude for the enjoyments of taste are long-faced, long-nosed and long-eyed; whatever their stature, they have something lanky about them. They have dark, lanky hair, and are never in good condition. It was one of them who invented trousers.

The Elixir of Youth Brillat-Savarin is equally certain as to the healthy benefits of good food:

A series of strictly exact observations has demonstrated that a succulent, delicate and choice diet delays for a long time and keeps aloof the external appearances of old age. It gives more brilliancy to the eye, more freshness to the skin, more support to the muscles; and as it is certain in physiology that it is the depression of the muscles that causes wrinkles, these formidable enemies of beauty (to which may be added 'flabbiness' and 'fleshiness'). It is equally true that, all things being equal, those who know how to eat are comparatively ten years younger than those ignorant of that science.

Truffles and Tumescence Among many other things, in *Physiologie du goût* Brillat-Savarin discusses the amorous effects of the truffle:

Whosoever pronounces the word *truffle* . . . awakens erotic and gastronomical dreams equally in that sex that wears skirts and the one that sprouts a beard.

The French had long had a proverb, advising that 'Those who desire to follow a virtuous path needs must leave truffles well alone.' There may be some basis for this belief: truffles contain androstenone, and scientific experiments have shown that if a dilute solution of this hormone is sprayed on men and women, both sexes become aroused. Androstenone is also found in men's armpits, and in pig's saliva; whether this latter fact has any bearing on the efficacy of pigs as truffle-hunters is not clear. What *is* clear, and indeed remarkable, is that people will pay over £1500 per kilogram for the finest white truffles, but nothing at all for odour of male armpit or for a mouthful of pig spit.

Bordeaux or Burgundy? Brillat-Savarin was once asked by a lady whether he preferred the wines of Bordeaux to those of Burgundy. 'That, Madame,' he told his interlocutor, 'is a question the answer to which I defer from concluding from week to week, such is the pleasure I take in the investigation.' He himself told the story of a wine lover who was offered grapes for dessert. 'Thank you so much,' the man replied, 'but I am not accustomed to take my wine in the form of pills.'

1826

Sheep's Head Celebrated In his journal, Sir Walter Scott expressed his loyalty to the cuisine of his native land: 'I wish for sheep's head and whisky toddy against all the French cookery and champagne in the world,' he wrote. Singed sheep's head was long regarded as a delicacy in Scotland, celebrated by poets from Francis Sempill to Robert Fergusson.

> An' there will be partans and buckies,
> And whitin's and speldin's enew,
> And singit sheep's heid, and a haggis,
> And scadlips to sup till ye spue.
>
> Francis Sempill (*circa* 1616–82), 'The Wedding
> of Maggie and Jock'

Scotland was not the only place to enjoy the dish: Florence used to have its *testicciolai* – butchers who specialized in sheep's heads.

The Scotch Haggis

In 1826 the Edinburgh journalist Mrs Isobel Johnstone published her *Cook and Housewife's Manual* under the pseudonym Margaret Dods – a nod towards the character of Meg Dods, the shrewish landlady of the Cleikum Inn in Sir Walter Scott's novel *St Ronan's Well* (1824). Among Mrs Johnstone's recommendations is that fish be 'ripened' for two or three days – perhaps reflecting the practice of the people of Lewis, in the Outer Hebrides, who would leave uncured skate hanging for the best part of a week before cooking it.

The Cook and Housewife's Manual became the most celebrated Scottish recipe book of the 19th century, and is particularly noted for its recipe for haggis:

Clean a sheep's pluck [heart, liver, lungs and windpipe] thoroughly.

Make incisions in the heart and liver to allow the blood to flow out, and parboil the whole, letting the wind-pipe lie over the side of the pot to permit the phlegm and blood to disgorge from the lungs; the water may be changed after a few minutes' boiling for fresh water.

A half-hour's boiling will be sufficient; but throw back the half of the liver to boil till it will grate easily; take the heart, the half of the liver, and part of the lights [lungs], trimming away all skins and black-looking parts, and mince them together.

Mince also a pound of good beef-suet and four onions. Grate the other half of the liver. Have a dozen of small onions peeled and scalded in two waters to mix with this mince.

Toast some oatmeal before the fire for hours, till it is of a light-brown colour and perfectly dry. Less than two-cupfuls of meal will do for this quantity of meat.

Spread the mince on a board, and strew the meal lightly over it, with a high seasoning of pepper, salt, and a little cayenne, well mixed.

Have a haggis-bag perfectly clean, and see that there be no thin part in it, else your whole labour will be lost by its bursting. Some cooks use two bags.

Put in the meat with a half-pint of good beef-gravy, or as much strong broth, as will make it a thick stew. Be careful not to fill the bag too full, but allow the meat room to swell; add the juice of a lemon, or a little good vinegar; press out the air, and sew up the bag; prick it with a large needle when it first swells in the pot, to prevent bursting; let it boil slowly for three hours if large.

~ ~ ~

1830

A New Foodstuff John Herschel, in *A Preliminary Discourse on the Study of Natural Philosophy*, advocated a new foodstuff, 'which renders famine next to impossible':

Who, for instance, would have conceived that . . . sawdust itself is susceptible of conversion into a substance bearing no remote analogy to bread; and though certainly less palatable than that of flour, yet no way disagreeable, and both wholesome and digestible as well as highly nutritative?

What Herschel did not realize was that wood, being around 50 per cent cellulose, is indigestible to humans – and to most animals, apart from termites.

1832

Sacher to the Rescue The Austrian statesman Prince Metternich put his kitchen staff into a panic when he ordered that they produce a new dessert for some special guests. The head chef was ill, but Metternich charged a 16-year-old apprentice called Franz Sacher with the task, declaring, 'Let there be no shame on me tonight!' Sacher came up trumps, improvising with what ingredients were to hand. The result: a chocolate sponge cake with apricot jam smeared between the layers and over the top and sides, all covered in a coating of dark chocolate, served with whipped cream. So was born the cake we know as Sachertorte. Thus goes the story, at any rate. In fact, the

Sachertorte in its present form, although based on Sacher's recipe, was perfected by Sacher's eldest son Eduard.

An Omelette is Born

In 1835, during the Carlist uprising in Spain, the rebels laid siege to Bilbao. One day during the siege, the Carlist commander, General Tomás de Zumalacárregui y de Imaz, was passing a farmhouse and demanded that the farmer's wife prepare him something to eat. All the woman had were some eggs, a potato and an onion, but she managed to rustle up what became a classic:

Cut some potatoes into thick slices, and roughly chop up an onion.

Heat a good dose of olive oil in a large frying pan, then gently fry the potatoes and onion until soft. Drain off the oil.

Beat the eggs and stir them into the potatoes and onion, and season.

Heat some of the reserved oil in another pan, and tip everything into it, shaping it all into a cushion shape with a spatula.

When almost set, slide the omelette onto a plate, turn it over, and return to the pan. Repeat this a few times until ready.

So delighted was the general with the result that he ordered the army caterers to make *tortilla de patatas* – what we call Spanish omelette – a standard part of the men's rations. So goes the story. In fact, the earliest description of the dish predates the Siege of Bilbao by a couple of decades.

— — —

1837

Bird's Custard Hatched A Birmingham pharmacist called Alfred Bird loved custard, but his wife was allergic to eggs, so he came up with an egg-free custard powder based on corn flour, to which one simply added milk – hence was born Bird's Custard, Britain's most popular brand. Bird's wife was also allergic to yeast – so he invented baking powder.

1838

The Origin of Worcestershire Sauce The Worcester grocers-cum-chemists Lea and Perrins launched their famous Worcestershire Sauce. Some time earlier in the decade they had been visited by an old India hand, whose identity they did not reveal, but whom they referred to as 'a nobleman in the county'. The nobleman had brought with him a scrap of paper with the recipe for his favourite Indian sauce, and asked Messrs Lea and Perrins to make up a large quantity. They found the result so hot that their eyes watered, but their client was well pleased. However, he did not want all that they had produced, and a number of barrels were left in storage. When they came to examine their stock a few years later, Lea and Perrins found it had benefited wonderfully from the maturation, and realized they had a money-spinner on their hands. Bottles of the stuff were even exported to India.

1839

How to Combat That Sinking Feeling

Francis Russell, Earl of Tavistock, succeeded his father as Duke of Bedford. His wife, Anna Maria, née Stanhope, is credited with the invention of that most British of meals, 'afternoon tea'. Over the years, the gap between breakfast and dinner had lengthened to such an extent that a light meal, 'luncheon', had been instituted in the 17th century to fill the gap (*see* 1652), but by the early 19th century dinner was not being served until seven o'clock in the evening, or even as late as half-past eight. This led the Duchess to complain of 'a

sinking feeling' somewhere around the late afternoon, and to remedy this she ordered her staff to serve tea accompanied by cakes at five o'clock.

Although afternoon tea has continued to appeal to the British, and was taken up by Parisian high society at the end of the 19th century, the institution greatly distressed the renowned chef Auguste Escoffier, who set up the celebrated kitchens at the Paris Ritz in 1898 and at the Carlton Hotel in London the following year. 'How can one eat jam, cakes and pastries, and enjoy a dinner – the king of meals – an hour or two later?' he plaintively reflected. 'How can one appreciate the food, the cooking or the wines?'

circa 1840

Do Not Blow Your Nose on the Tablecloth One anonymous writer on etiquette advised that 'Ladies may wipe their lips on the tablecloth, but not blow their noses on it.'

On the Tolerableness of Peas The Regency dandy Beau Brummell, known for his aversion to vegetables, died. Once, when asked whether he had indeed ever eaten anything of a vegetable nature, he pondered a while then responded, 'I once ate a pea.' On another occasion, questioned as to why he had failed to marry a particular lady, he replied, 'Why, what could I do, my good fellow, but cut the connection? I discovered that Lady Mary actually ate cabbage!'

A Surfeit of Coffee An epitaph on a gravestone in Connecticut reads:

> Here lies, cut down like unripe fruit,
> The wife of Deacon Amos Shute.
> She died of drinking too much coffee,
> Anny Dominy, eighteen forty.

Bombay Duck The British in Bombay (Mumbai) delighted in a local garnish made from a small fish called the bummalo, which were seasoned with asafoetida, dried in the sun, fried until crispy and then crumbled over food. Apparently the Bombay British adopted the name 'duck' for the fish as they swim near the surface, while 'Bombay' is a play on 'bummalo'. Such was their enthusiasm for the garnish that the British of Bombay themselves became known as 'Ducks'.

1842

The Ideal Number for a Dinner Party In *The Blue Belles of England*, Fanny Trollope stated that the number for a dinner party 'must neither be less than the graces [three], nor more than the muses [nine]'. When, a century or so later, the wealthy industrialist and philanthropist Nubar Gulbenkian was asked what the best number for a dinner party was, he replied, 'Two. Myself and a damned good head waiter.'

1843

British Food Part Three: Flat, Stale and Unprofitable In his novel *Handley Cross*, R.S. Surtees gives the following account of the typical British catering establishment of the period:

Now for a chop house or coffee-room dinner! Oh, the 'orrible smell that greets you at the door! Compound of cabbage, pickled salmon, boiled beef, saw-dust, and anchovy sarce . . . everything tastes flat, stale, and unprofitable.

1845

A Horrible Barbarity In her influential *Modern Cookery for Private Families*, Eliza Acton offered the following regrettable advice regarding the cooking of vegetables:

> Vegetables when not sufficiently cooked are known to be exceedingly unwholesome and indigestible, that the custom of serving them crisp, which means, in reality, only half-boiled, should be altogether disregarded . . . when health is considered more important than fashion.

She was in other aspects more enlightened, for example condemning the then common practice of skinning and cutting up eels while they were still alive as a 'horrible barbarity'. And those who scrape a living by scribbling will sympathize with her contrasting recipes for 'Poor Author's Pudding' and 'The Publisher's Pudding', which 'can scarcely be made *too rich*'.

Miss Acton, already a poet of modest reputation, had originally approached her publisher with a manuscript of 'further fugitive verses', only to be told that they would prefer a cookery book. The result was *Modern Cookery*, a Victorian classic that remained in print for the rest of the century.

— — —

The Welcome Guest's Own Pudding

The 'author's receipt' for this 'light and wholesome' dessert comes from Eliza Acton's classic *Modern Cookery for Private Families* (1845):

Pour, quite boiling, on four ounces of fine bread crumbs, an exact half-pint of new milk, or of thin cream; lay a plate over the basin and let them remain until cold.

Then stir to them four ounces of dry crumbs of bread, four of very finely minced beef-kidney suet, a small pinch of salt, three ounces of coarsely crushed ratafias, three ounces of candied citron and orange-rind sliced thin, and the grated rind of one large or of two small lemons.

Clear, and whisk four large eggs well, throw to them by degrees four ounces of powdered sugar, and continue to whisk them until it is dissolved, and they are very light; stir them to, and beat them well up with the other ingredients.

Pour the mixture into a thickly buttered mould, or basin which will contain nearly a quart, and which it should fill to within half an inch of brim; lay first a buttered paper, then a well floured pudding-cloth over the top, tie them tightly and very securely round, gather up and fasten the corners of the cloth, and boil the pudding for two hours at the utmost.

Let it stand for a minute or two before it is dished, and serve it with simple wine sauce . . . or with pine-apple or any other *clear* fruit sauce.

A Recipe for Stewed Duke The Duke of Norfolk came in for considerable vilification for suggesting that the poor of Ireland, then suffering from the terrible potato famine, might blunt their hunger by taking a little curry powder. An anonymous wag from the Beefsteak Club in London wrote to *The Times* as follows:

Sir, – As I cannot doubt your sympathy with your poorer countrymen, in the event of a scarcity, I beg to send you my receipt for dressing a very simple dish:–

NORFOLK CURRY

Take a duke, no matter how foolish, but the fatter the better, stew him down with 'peppers, and a variety of things of that description,' and serve him up as the principal dish at an agricultural meeting – any fool can cut him up.

This is a very warm dish to the stomach; if 'not palatable at first,' wash it down with a glass or two of milk punch.

Yours truly,

HANNAH GLASSE.

(Hannah Glasse's *The Art of Cookery Made Plain and Easy*, published in 1747, had been the first English book to provide recipes for curries.) For its part, *Punch* magazine carried a spoof brochure, supposedly penned by the duke, entitled 'How to live on a pinch of curry':

Take a saucepan, or, if you have not one, borrow one. Throw in about a gallon of good water, and let it warm over a fire till it boils. Now be ready with your curry, which you may keep in a snuff box if you like, and take a pinch of it. Pop the pinch into the hot water, and serve it out, before going to bed, to your hungry children.

1847

Invention of the Ring Doughnut According to a popular legend (which may or may not be true), the first ring doughnut was created by Hansen Gregory, a 15-year-old baker's apprentice aboard a US merchantman, when, using the ship's tin pepper box, he knocked the soggy centre out of a doughnut he had just fried. Un-ringed doughnuts had been around for several decades by this time – Washington Irving referred in his 1809 *History of New York* to 'balls of sweetened dough, fried in hog's fat, and called doughnuts'. In 1939 at the New York World's Fair there was exhibited a model of a proposed 300-foot statue to Hansen Gregory, in honour of his achievement. The statue was to be erected on Mount Battie in Maine, and (if it had ever been built) would have been visible from 50 miles away.

French Food Part Two: Frogs and Old Gloves In R.H. Barham's poem 'The Bagman's Dog' (from *The Ingoldsby Legends*), we read of British suspicions of French food:

'Hot, smoking hot,' on the fire was a pot
Well replenish'd, but really I can't say with what,
For, famed as the French always are for ragouts,
No creature can tell what they put in their stews,
Whether bull-frogs, old gloves, or old wigs, or old
shoes.

Another culinary item that met with Barham's disapproval was the cucumber:

'Tis not her coldness, father,
That chills my labouring breast;
It's that confounded cucumber
I've ate and can't digest.

'The Confession'

The Result of Austrian Vegetable Cookery While staying in Paris at the home of a former colleague, Friedrich Engels wrote to Karl Marx to complain:

The stench is like five thousand unaired feather beds, multiplied by the release therein of innumerable farts – the result of Austrian vegetable cookery.

Becky Sharp and the Chilli At one point in Thackeray's novel *Vanity Fair* (published in serial form in 1847–8), the ambitious Becky Sharp sets her sights on Jos Sedley, an East India Company nabob. One evening, when dining with Sedley and his parents, she has her first experience of Anglo-Indian cuisine:

'Give Miss Sharp some curry, my dear,' said Mr Sedley, laughing.

Rebecca had never tasted the dish before.

'Do you find it as good as everything else from India?' said Mr Sedley.

'Oh, excellent!' said Rebecca, who was suffering tortures with the cayenne pepper.

'Try a chilli with it, Miss Sharp,' said Joseph, really interested.

'A chilli,' said Rebecca, gasping. 'Oh yes!' She thought a chilli was something cool, as its name imported, and was served with some. 'How fresh and green they look,' she said, and put one into her mouth. It was hotter than the curry; flesh and blood could bear it no longer. She laid down her fork. 'Water, for Heaven's sake, water!' she cried. Mr Sedley burst out laughing (he was a coarse man, from the Stock Exchange, where they love all sorts of practical jokes). 'They are real Indian, I assure you,' said he. 'Sambo, give Miss Sharp some water.'

Thackeray himself had been born in India, and acquired a taste for its cuisine from various aunts and uncles who had spent time out there. He even wrote a poem to curry, which he held to be 'A dish for Emperors to feed upon'.

1848

On the Importance of Dumplings The inbred and incapable Ferdinand I abdicated as emperor of Austria. His father in his will had decreed that his son, if he was to succeed to the throne, would have to consult his Uncle Louis and Prince Metternich before doing anything at all. When Ferdinand tried to consummate his marriage with Princess Maria Anna of Sardinia he suffered five seizures, after which he appears to have given up. To amuse himself he would roll around in wastepaper baskets and try to catch flies with his bare hands. His most masterly moment came when the palace chef informed him that regrettably he could not serve the emperor any apricot dumplings, as apricots were not in season. To this Ferdinand famously retorted, 'I am the emperor, and I want dumplings!' Ferdinand lived on until 1875.

circa 1850

The Pleasures of Civet Poo After the colonial authorities in the Dutch East Indies prohibited native farmers and plantation workers from picking coffee berries for their own consumption, the locals found a cunning way around the letter of the law. Having noticed that the *luwak*, the palm civet, ate the berries for the soft pulp and then excreted the undigested seeds in their droppings, they collected the seeds, which they then washed, roasted and ground to make a particularly delicious beverage – known as *kopi luwak*. *Kopi luwak* is vividly aromatic and yet much less bitter than other coffees, a result of the chemical effect on the beans of certain enzymes in the civet's stomach. The reputation of civet-processed coffee soon spread to the plantation owners themselves, and today *kopi luwak* is the most expensive coffee in the world, selling at up to $600 per pound.

Entirely Taken Up in the Pursuit of his Personal Gratifications The last nawab of Oudh, Wajid Ali Shah, played a trick on his dinner guest, Prince Mirza Asman of Delhi, by having his cook disguise a dish of meat korma as a murrabba, a spicy vegetable conserve. The prince, who prided himself as something of connoisseur when it came to matters gastronomic, was completely taken in. Some time later he issued a return invitation to the nawab in order to get his own back. When the nawab sat down to eat, he was disconcerted to find that every dish he tasted – the rice, the curries, the kebabs, the bread and even the pickles – all consisted of just one ingredient: caramelized sugar.

The nawabs of Oudh had long been famous for their patronage of the gastronomic arts. In the early 1770s it was reported that Nawab Shuja-ud-Daula was spending four times as much on his cook as he was on his poor house, and guests at the nawab's table could expect such delicious tricks as almonds carved into the shapes of grains of rice and pistachios cut into the form of lentils. Shuja's successor, Asaf-ud-Daula, surpassed him in gluttony: despite having lost all his teeth, he grew so fat he could not ride a horse. According to tradition, to keep the tooth-less nawab's hunger at bay his well-paid cook had come up with shammi kebabs, which are made out of such finely minced and pounded meat that they do not require either biting or chewing.

This sort of frivolity was frowned upon by the British, who had long had their eyes on Oudh. In 1855 William Knighton wrote in *The Private Life of an Eastern King*, his unflattering portrait of Wajid Ali Shah:

> He is entirely taken up in the pursuit of his personal gratifications. He has no desire to be thought to take any interest whatever in public affairs and is alto-gether regardless of the duties and responsibilities of his high office. He lives exclusively in the society of fiddlers, eunuchs and women: he has done so since his childhood, and is likely to do so till his last.

The nawab was duly sent into exile in 1856, and his terri-tory annexed by the British.

An Antipodean Feast

In *Our Antipodes*, a work by G.C. Mundy published in 1852, the author gives an account of a dinner party held in Sydney, Australia, at which the following dishes were served:

Wallabi-tail soup

A slice of boiled schnapper, with oyster sauce

A delicate wing of the wonga-wonga pigeon and bread sauce

A dessert of plantains and loquots, guavas and mandarin oranges, pomegranates and cherimoyas

All this, Mundy says, 'helped to convince me I was not in Belgravia'.

1853

Revenge is a Dish Best Served . . . Deep-fried On 24 August, George 'Speck' Crum, chef at Moon's Lake House at Saratoga Springs, New York, was so annoyed when a diner complained that his French fries were 'too thick' that he took a new batch of potatoes and sliced them as thin as sheets of paper before deep-frying them until they were dry and crisp right through. He was convinced that the irritating diner would find them completely inedible – but, to the contrary, the man found them quite delicious. And so potato chips – or crisps, as the British call them – were born. At least that is the story, but it seems that recipes for something similar were already in existence by this time.

How the Eskimo Eats Elisha Kane, a medical officer in the US Navy, embarked on an expedition to try to discover the whereabouts of Sir John Franklin, lost somewhere in the Arctic in search of the Northwest Passage. In the course of his search Kane and his men penetrated further north than any previous expedition had succeeded in doing. While in the Arctic he stayed with an Inuit family in an igloo, and later described in *Arctic Explorations* (1857) their method of eating raw meat:

> They cut the meat in long strips, introduced one end into the mouth, swallowed it as far as the powers of deglutition would allow, and then, cutting off the protruding portion close to the lips, prepared themselves for a second mouthful. It was really a feat of address: those of us who tried it failed awkwardly; and yet I have seen infants in the mother's hood, not

two years old, who managed to perform it without incident.

Polar Bear's Liver While in the Arctic Dr Kane initially dismissed as a 'vulgar prejudice' the Inuit warning that the liver of the polar bear is poisonous, but in his journal for 8 October 1853 he notes:

> The cub's liver was my supper last night, and today I have the symptoms of poison in full measure – vertigo, diarrhoea and their concomitants.

The toxicity of polar bear's liver is due to the high concentration of vitamin A it contains. If eaten at a single sitting, between 30 and 90 grams of liver is sufficient to kill a human being.

Nesselrode Pudding

While in Paris in 1856 to negotiate the treaty that ended the Crimean War, the Russian foreign minister Count Karl Robert Nesselrode was honoured by a new dish. 'Nesselrode pudding', devised by the count's French chef Monsieur Mony, is a frozen dessert whose ingredients were intended to reflect aspects of Nesselrode himself: chestnuts for his Westphalian ancestry, raisins for his birthplace in Lisbon, and Greek currants to represent his enmity towards the Turks.

An early version of the recipe was supplied by Jules Gouffé in *The Royal Pastry and Confectionery Book*, published in London in 1874:

Peel 40 fine Italian chestnuts, blanch them in boiling water to remove the second skin, and put them in a stewpan with 1 quart of syrup registering 16° and a stick of vanilla;

Simmer gently until the chestnuts are done, drain, and rub them through a hair sieve;

Mix in a stewpan 8 yolks of egg and a half lb. of powdered sugar, add 1 quart of boiled cream, and stir over the fire, without boiling, until the egg begins to thicken, mix in the chestnut purée and 1 gill of Maraschino, and strain the whole through a tammy-cloth into a basin;

Set a freezing-pot in the ice;

Wash and dry a quarter lb. of currants, and boil them up in some syrup registering 30°;

Stone a quarter lb. of raisins, cut them in halves, and boil them in syrup in the same way;

Pour the chestnut cream in the freezing-pot, work it with the spatula until it is partly frozen, add 3 gills of whipped double cream, continue working until the cream is frozen, and mix in the prepared fruit, previously drained;

Put the ice in a dome-shaped ice-mould, and finish as directed in the preceding recipe.

When first invented, this pudding was frozen in a bladder instead of in a mould.

Sauce for Nesselrode Pudding

Put 4 yolks of egg in a stewpan with a quarter lb. of pounded sugar and 3 gills of boiled cream, stir over the fire, without boiling, until the egg begins to thicken, take the stewpan off the fire, and stir for three minutes more;

Strain the sauce through a tammy-cloth into a stewpan, add a gill of Maraschino and put the stewpan in the ice, so that the sauce may be very cold, but not frozen, and serve it in a boat with the pudding.

1855

Charcoal Biscuits James Bird, in his book *Vegetable Charcoal: Its Medicinal and Economic Properties with Practical Remarks on Its Use in Chronic Affections of the Stomach and Bowels*, recommends charcoal biscuits as the best way of administering charcoal to children. Charcoal biscuits, which were first made in the early 19th century as a treatment for flatulence, were made from flour, butter, sugar, eggs and charcoal derived from willow wands. They continued to be popular into the 20th century.

1857

Pink Lemonade In America a certain Pete Conklin came up with a novelty drink: pink lemonade. The secret ingredient was a bucket of water in which a horse rider had soaked his red tights.

1859

On the Consumption of Mermaids In *The Curiosities of Food; or the Dainties and Delicacies of Different Nations Obtained from the Animal Kingdom*, Peter Lund Simmonds described how the meat of the manatee, a large marine mammal apparently frequently mistaken by sailors for a mermaid, was a delicacy in the West Indies, its flesh being as white and as tasty as pork. However, Simmonds could not help but anthropomorphize. 'It appears horrible,' he wrote, 'to chew and swallow the flesh of an animal which holds its young (it has never more than one at a litter) to its breast, which is formed exactly like that of a woman, with paws resembling human hands.'

Rats as a Delicacy

In the same book, Simmonds wrote of the culinary value attached to the rat by the Chinese, especially those who had migrated to California:

> In China, rat soup is considered equal to oxtail soup, and a dozen fine rats will realize two dollars, or eight or nine shillings.
>
> Besides the attractions of the gold fields for the Chinese, California is so abundantly supplied with rats, that they can live like celestial emperors, and pay very little for their board . . . Their professed cooks, we are told, serve up rats' brains in a much superior style to the Roman dish of nightingales' and peacocks' tongues. The sauce used is garlic, aromatic seeds and camphor.

1860

A Favourite Atrocity of the English Kitchen The tradition of cooking green vegetables with bicarbonate of soda was roundly condemned by the renowned Tabitha Tickletooth in her book, *The Dinner Question; or, How to Dine Well & Economically*. 'Never,' thunders Miss Tickletooth,

> Never under any circumstances, unless you wish entirely to destroy all flavour, and reduce your peas to a pulp, boil them with soda. This favourite atrocity of the English kitchen cannot be too strongly condemned.

The practice, which goes back to Roman times and was long prevalent in Britain and North America, enhances the greenness of the vegetables, but also makes them limp, and destroys vitamins B_1 and C.

Tabitha Tickletooth was the nom de plume of a Victorian actor and drag artist whose real name was Charles Selby (*circa* 1802–63). *The Dinner Question* is full of sound advice about getting the basics right, and advises its readers not to fret too much about fancy presentation. For example:

> The late Lord Dudley truly said, 'A good soup, a small turbot, a neck of venison, and an apricot tart,

is a dinner fit for an emperor.' Let, then, your dinner be based on this principle, for in proportion to its smallness ought to be its excellence both as to the quality of its materials and its cookery.

Experimental Zoophagy In London, the newly formed Acclimatization Society held its first dinner. The menu featured such delicacies as sea slug, kangaroo and curassow – for the purpose of the society was to establish which exotic species might be successfully bred in Britain for the table. Presiding over the occasion was the naturalist and experimental zoophage Frank Buckland, who had, as a boy, been introduced by his father, the Reverend William Buckland, to a range of unconventional fare, from squirrel pie and mice in batter to horse tongue and ostrich. Buckland *père* himself, a distinguished geologist and canon of Christ Church, Oxford, claimed to have eaten the embalmed heart of Louis XIV. While Buckland *fils* was himself at Oxford, he embarked on his own gastronomic experiments, starting with the recently deceased panther at the Surrey Zoological Gardens, which was disinterred at his request. 'It was not very good,' he later confessed. Among the other beasts subjected to Buckland's bold palate were rhinoceros ('like very tough beef'), porpoise ('broiled lamp-wick'), elephant trunk ('rubbery') and giraffe ('like veal'). The common mole he declared to be 'utterly horrible', being only surpassed in awfulness by the bluebottle.

The First Fish and Chip Shop in England Although Marranos – Jewish exiles from Portugal – had introduced fried fish to England in the 16th century, it was not until 1860 that Joseph Malin, a Jewish immigrant from Eastern Europe, began to sell fried fish alongside chipped potatoes at his establishment in London's East End. In 1968 Malin's of Bow was honoured by the National Federation of Fish Fryers with a plaque commemorating their role in establishing the archetypal British 'chippy'. At much the same time in Lancashire, the existing tradition of chip shops was joined by fried fish, whose import to the big cities was aided by the spread of the railways. John Lees of Mossley, Greater Manchester, is credited with opening the first fish and chip shop in the North in 1863.

By the late 1920s, there were some 35,000 fish and chip shops across Britain – and the popularity of fish and chips, combined with its nutritional value as a good source of protein, vitamins and carbohydrates, meant that it remained unrationed throughout the Second World War. Today, there are fewer than 9000 chippies in Britain, but at the beginning of the 21st century they were still selling some 250 million meals a year.

Resurrection Cheeses In the 1979 issue of *The Carmarthenshire Historian*, Major Francis Jones, Wales Herald of Arms Extraordinary, described the provenance of the famous 'Resurrection cheeses' once made at Trefenty, near St Clears in South Wales:

> About the years 1860–64, Mr Plowden permitted a shepherd to keep two cows on the demesne. Their milk enabled him to make cheese which he sold to augment his scanty wages. As he could not afford to buy a cheese-press *(peis)* the enterprising fellow went to the deserted churchyard [of Llanfihangel Aber-cywyn] and took a few of the fallen headstones, and with deftness and ingenuity fashioned the necessary article, which despite its homely construction proved thoroughly efficient. Farmhouse cheeses in those days were large and circular, often well over a foot, even two feet, in diameter, as delicious to the taste as nutritious for the system. Now, one of the stones used by the adroit shepherd bore the inscription 'In memory of David Thomas', and those words came out clearly etched on the cheeses. He carried them to St Clears and it was not long before he attracted customers, one of whom having read the inscription on his purchase, observed 'You have resurrected this cheese from Llanfihangel churchyard!' This caused much mirth, and thereafter the succulent produce of Trefenty became known throughout the district as 'the Resurrection Cheese' – *caws yr Atgyfodiad*.

1861

How to Butcher a Turtle In the recipe for turtle soup in her *Book of Household Management*, Mrs Beeton gives the following instructions for how to butcher one's turtle:

> To make this soup with less difficulty, cut off the head of the turtle the preceding day. In the morning open the turtle by leaning heavily with a knife on the shell of the animal's back, whilst you cut this off all round. Turn it upright on its end, that all the water, &c. may run out, when the flesh should be cut off along the spine, with the knife sloping towards the bones, for fear of touching the gall, which sometimes might escape the eye. When all the flesh about the members is obtained, wash these clean, and let them drain . . .

As André Launay observes in *Caviare and After* (1964), 'getting the meat from a turtle is similar to decarbonizing an engine'.

Although a delicacy in Victorian England, turtle (of the large freshwater kind) was a staple in parts of Brazil, as explained in *The Naturalist on the River Amazon* (1863) by Henry Walter Bates (best remembered for his account of mimicry in animals):

The flesh is very tender, palatable and wholesome; but it is very cloying; every one ends, sooner or later, by becoming thoroughly surfeited. I became so sick of turtle in the course of two years that I could not bear the smell of it, although at the same time nothing else was to be had, and I was suffering actual hunger.

Bates goes on to describe the various ways in which the native women cook the meat:

The entrails are chopped up and made into a delicious soup called sarapatel, which is generally boiled in the concave upper shell of the animal used as a kettle. The tender flesh of the breast is partially minced with farinha [cassava], and the breast shell then roasted over the fire, making a very pleasant dish. Large sausages are made of the thick-coated stomach, which is filled with minced meat and boiled. The quarters cooked in Tucupi sauce form another variety of food. When surfeited with turtle in all other shapes, pieces of the lean part roasted on a spit and moistened only with vinegar make an agreeable change.

The Full English

'The following list of hot dishes,' wrote Mrs Beeton in her *Book of Household Management* (1861), 'may perhaps assist our readers in knowing what to provide for the comfortable meal called breakfast.'

Broiled fish
such as mackerel, whiting, herrings, dried
haddocks, &c.

Mutton chops and rump-steaks

Broiled sheep's kidneys

Kidneys à la maître d'hôtel

Sausages

Plain rashers of bacon

Bacon and poached eggs

Ham and poached eggs

Omelettes

Plain boiled eggs

Oeufs-au-plat

Poached eggs on toast

Muffins, toast, marmalade, butter, &c. &c.

No wonder Somerset Maugham pronounced that 'To eat well in England, all you have to do is take breakfast three times a day.'

— —

Collared Calf's Head

The following recipe is a typical offering from Mrs Beeton's *Book of Household Management* (1861). Prior to one's calf being slaughtered, the author advises that 'if the weather is fine and genial, [the calf] should be turned into an orchard or small paddock for a few hours each day, to give it an opportunity to acquire a relish for the fresh pasture'.

Mode. – Scald the head for a few minutes; take it out of the water, and with a blunt knife scrape off all the hair.

Clean it nicely, divide the head and remove the brains. Boil it tender enough to take out the bones, which will be about 2 hours.

When the head is boned, flatten it on the table, sprinkle over it a thick layer of parsley, then a layer of ham, and then the yolks of the [6 hard-boiled] eggs cut into thin rings and put a seasoning of pounded mace, nutmeg, and white pepper between each layer; roll the head up in a cloth, and tie it up as tight as possible.

Boil it for 4 hours, and when it is taken out of the pot, place a heavy weight on the top, the same as for other collars.

Let it remain till cold; then remove the cloth and binding, and it will be ready to serve.

— — —

Squashed Flies To honour the popular Italian nationalist leader Giuseppe Garibaldi, Peek Frean and Co of Bermondsey, London, named their new biscuit in his honour. These flat rectangular biscuits with a currant filling are still known as Garibaldi Biscuits – or, more popularly, as 'squashed flies' or 'fly cemeteries'.

1865

Duelling with Sausages So angered was the Prussian chancellor, Otto von Bismarck, by the criticisms of his large military budget made by the liberal politician and pioneering pathologist Rudolf Virchow, that he challenged his opponent to a duel. Virchow, being given the choice of weapons, told the chancellor that he had two sausages: one completely healthy, and one infected with botulism – a disease that often proves fatal. He invited Bismarck to choose first which he would eat; he himself would then eat the other. The chancellor, both amused and horrified, withdrew his challenge.

The *Banquet Hippophagique* In an effort to promote horseflesh to the French working classes as an affordable alternative to beef and pork, a great *banquet hippophagique* ('horse-eating feast') was held in Paris, featuring such dishes as horse consommé, horse sausages and horse à la mode. Although French troops during the Napoleonic Wars had in dire circumstances sometimes resorted to eating horseflesh, the meat of horses was not popular in France – Edmond de Goncourt described it as 'watery and blackish red,' while Alexandre Dumas doubted whether it would ever catch on. However, in 1866 the French government licensed specialist horse butchers, and the Siege of Paris in 1870–1 did much to boost consumption. Subsequently, the *boucherie chevaline* became a feature on most French high streets, advertised by a sculpted horse head over the door, while within the carcases were decorated with ribbons and artificial flowers. Such butchers are now an increasingly rare sight, as consumption of horseflesh in France has suffered a marked decline in recent decades.

1866

Ode on the Mammoth Cheese Weighing Over 7000 Pounds This is the title of the most celebrated poem by James McIntyre, the amateur Canadian versifier known as 'the Cheese Poet'. The cheese in question was produced in his home town of Ingersoll, Ontario, and displayed at exhibitions in Toronto, New York and Great Britain. Here is McIntyre's acknowledged masterpiece in its entirety:

> We have seen thee, Queen of cheese,
> Laying quietly at your ease,
> Gently fanned by evening breeze –
> Thy fair form no flies dare seize.

> All gaily dressed soon you'll go
> To the great Provincial Show,
> To be admired by many a beau
> In the city of Toronto.

> Cows numerous as a swarm of bees –
> Or as the leaves upon the trees –
> It did require to make thee please,
> And stand unrivalled Queen of Cheese.

> May you not receive a scar as
> We have heard that Mr Harris
> Intends to send you off as far as
> The great World's Show at Paris.

> Of the youth – beware of these –
> For some of them might rudely squeeze
> And bite your cheek; then songs or glees
> We could not sing o' Queen of Cheese.

> We 'rt thou suspended from balloon,
> You'd cast a shade, even at noon;
> Folks would think it was the moon
> About to fall and crush them soon.

McIntyre was born in Scotland in 1828, and emigrated to Canada in 1841, eventually settling in Ingersoll, where he set up as a cabinet-and-coffin maker, and also as an undertaker. He became the laureate of the country's infant cheese industry, penning such immortal lines as these:

> The ancient poets ne'er did dream
> That Canada was land of cream,
> They ne'er imagined it could flow
> In this cold land of ice and snow,
> Where everything did solid freeze
> They ne'er hoped or looked for cheese.

McIntyre's work occasionally featured in the Toronto *Globe*, and he published two volumes in his lifetime, continuing to write up until his death in 1906. Today, the town of Ingersoll holds an annual poetry competition in his honour, in which entrants must versify on the subject of . . . cheese. Just outside Ingersoll, at the junction of highways 19 and 401, the Ontario Archaeological and Historical Sites Board has erected a monument to 'The big cheese of 1866'.

1867

The Smelliest Cheese in the World? The first Limburger cheese was created in his cellar by Rudolph Benkerts, in the former Duchy of Limburg (now divided between the Netherlands, Germany and Belgium). The notorious smell of this semi-hard white goat's cheese is generated by the microorganism used in the fermentation process, *Brevibacterium linens*, which is also responsible for human foot odour. In 2006 a scientific study showed that the mosquito that spreads malaria is equally attracted to the smell of Limburger and the smell of human feet.

Lobster as a Weapon of War In his invaluable *Crab, Shrimp and Lobster Lore*, W.B. Lord described the curious uses to which tinned lobster has been put:

It has been said that during the Indian war [presumably the 1857 Mutiny] a box of regimental stores belonging to our forces fell into the hands of the enemy, who thinking that a great capture of some kind of deadly and destructive ammunition had been made, rammed the painted tin cases, with goodly charges of powder behind them, into their immense guns, laid them steadily on the devoted British troops, and then with a flash and a thundering roar, preserved lobster, from Fortnum and Mason's, was scattered far and wide over the battlefield.

One Last Missionary for the Pot The Reverend Thomas Baker, a missionary from Playden in Sussex, committed a regrettable social solecism by pulling a comb from the hair of the local chief while proselytizing in the Navosa Highlands of Viti Levu, Fiji. The outraged inhabitants thereupon set upon the reverend gentleman with an axe, chopped him into pieces, then cooked and ate him, along with seven of his Fijian disciples. Baker is said to have been the last missionary eaten in Fiji.

To Europeans, Fiji was then known as the Cannibal Isles, as cannibalism had supposedly been a standard component of inter-tribal warfare for centuries. In the early 19th century, one chief, Ratu Udre Udre, was reputed to have eaten 872 people, and to have raised a line of stones, one for every victim, to celebrate his achievement. According to his son, Udre Udre prided himself on eating every part of his victims, including the head, and saving anything he couldn't eat at one banquet for the next. It was apparently customary to deploy a 14-tined fork during cannibalistic feasts, and for tribespeople to greet their chief with the phrase, 'Eat me!'

Such traditions, and Baker's unfortunate end, inspired 'The Whale Tooth', Jack London's 1911 short story about a missionary among 'the frizzle-headed man-eaters' of Fiji:

The missionary was surrounded by a mass of naked savages, all struggling to get at him. The death song, which is the song of the oven, was raised, and his expostulations could no longer be heard . . .

Today Fijians, largely Christian converts, regard their cannibalistic past as *Na gauna ni tevoro*, 'the time of the devil', and in 2003 the chief of the clan responsible for Baker's demise formally apologized to his descendants.

1868

A Love of Music and Food Part Two: Tournedos Rossini

The Italian opera composer Gioacchino Rossini, who was also a noted gourmand and a renowned amateur chef, died. The famous tournedos Rossini – thin slices of fillet steak fried in butter and topped with foie gras, served on a crouton with a Madeira demi-glace sauce and garnished with slices of black truffle – was said by some to have been created posthumously in his honour by the great French chef Auguste Escoffier. Others credit Escoffier's famous precursor Antonin Carême, or Cassimir Moisson, chef at the Maison Dorée. There is a also a story that Rossini himself was responsible, as related by Pamela Joan Vandyke Price in *France: A Food and Wine Guide* (1966):

Rossini was dining at the Café Anglais and . . . suggested an alternative method of cutting and preparing the steak . . . The horrified *maître d'hotel* announced that he could not present a dish that was unpresentable. 'Very well,' said Rossini, 'then don't let us see you do it – I'll turn my back' (*tourne le dos*).

Truffles were one of Rossini's favourite ingredients, named by him 'the Mozart of mushrooms'. The composer claimed only to have ever cried three times in his adult life: once when he heard the virtuoso violinist Niccolò Paganini, once when his first opera was received with cat calls, and once when, while taking a picnic on a boat, a chicken stuffed with truffles was lost overboard.

Rossini's gargantuan appetite is attested by the story that at the end of a dinner party featuring some particularly excellent dishes, the hostess turned to him and asked when he would dine with them again. 'Right away!' Rossini replied.

1869

Divided Opinions on the Durian The durian fruit of Southeast Asia has elicited a variety of responses, from devoted enthusiasm to complete and utter revulsion. The naturalist Alfred Russel Wallace was in the former camp, as he describes in *The Malay Archipelago* (1869):

> A rich butter-like custard highly flavoured with almonds gives the best general idea of it, but inter-mingled with it comes wafts of flavour that call to mind cream-cheese, onion-sauce, brown-sherry, and other incongruities. Then there is a rich glutinous smoothness in the pulp which nothing else possesses, but which adds to its delicacy. It is neither acid, nor sweet, nor juicy, yet one feels the want of none of these qualities, for it is perfect as it is. It produces no nausea nor other bad affect, and the more you eat of it the less you feel inclined to stop. In fact, to eat durians is a new sensation worth a voyage to the East to experience.

Others have compared eating the fruit to the consumption of sewage, rotten onions, stale vomit, gym socks or surgical swabs, and such is its smell that its carriage is forbidden on all public transport in Indonesia. One traveller who was in the anti-camp was the physician Victor Heiser, who in *An American Doctor's Odyssey in Forty-Five Countries* (1936) recounts the following instructive anecdote:

With a friend, I was on a tram from Bangkok to Penang. During a stop at a station the only other occupant of the compartment, a Chinese, bought a durian and proceeded to cut it in half. Almost overpowered by the smell, we called the guard and asked him to persuade our travelling companion to eat his durian on the platform, which he obligingly did. We had just begun to eat our ham sandwiches when he returned and started to make gestures of repulsion, shook his head and ejaculated 'Whew! Whew! Whew!' as though he was overcome with disgust. Then he, too, called the guard to whom he spoke in Malay. The guard turned to us and asked if we would mind stepping outside to eat our lunch. Since the Chinese had been so polite in acceding to our request we felt we could do no less than return the favour. To a final 'Whew!' we also left. When we had finished our innocent sandwiches and returned the jocular Chinese looked up with a broad grin on his face.

1870

The Great Spinach Myth In the published results of his measurements of the iron content of spinach, the German scientist Dr Emil von Wolff misplaced a decimal point, giving the vegetable a tenfold increase over the actual figure, and a reputation for increasing the strength of anyone who ate it – iron being crucial to the manufacture of red blood cells. Hence spinach became the favourite food of the mighty-muscled comic-strip character created by Elzie Crisler Segar in January 1929, a character whose theme song goes:

> I'm Popeye the Sailor Man,
> I'm Popeye the Sailor Man,
> I'm strong to the finich
> Cause I eats me spinach,
> I'm Popeye the Sailor Man.

Consumption of spinach in the USA rose over 30 per cent as a consequence of Popeye's endorsement. However, in 1937 German chemists uncovered Dr Wolff's error, and it was realized that spinach is no richer in iron than most other green vegetables.

That, at least, is the commonly repeated account, but in 2010 Dr Mike Sutton of Nottingham Trent University published a paper in the *Internet Journal of Criminology* in which he concluded, after extensive research, that he could find no mention of Dr Wolff's misplaced decimal point in any published source, academic or otherwise, earlier than

1981. Sutton established that in some versions of the story the scientist was not Wolff but Gustav von Bunge, who in 1890 is said to have given rise to the error by measuring the iron content of dried spinach, which has a much higher iron concentration than fresh spinach. What's more, it turns out that Segar chose spinach as the source of Popeye's power not because of its iron content, but because it is high in vitamin A. For example, in a strip dated 3 July 1932, Popeye is seen chomping spinach straight from the vegetable bed, while declaring 'Spinach is full of vitamin "A" an' tha's what makes hoomans strong an' helty.' In none of the hundreds of old cartoons studied by Sutton is there any association made between spinach and iron.

As it turns out, most of the iron in spinach is bound by oxalic acid in an insoluble salt, so no more than 5 per cent of it can be absorbed during digestion. Segar certainly realized that spinach and other greens are full of vitamins and wished to promote their consumption to both adults and children; hitherto, such vegetables had been regarded as animal food. There was clearly some resistance, as the famous 1935 cartoon by Carl Rose attests:

Mother: It's broccoli, dear.
Child: I say it's spinach, and I say to hell with it.

A Parisian Siege Menu

During the winter of 1870–1, as the four-month siege of Paris by the Prussian army tightened, the beleaguered citizens resorted to all kinds of novel foods to keep themselves from starvation. Henry Labouchère, the correspondent for the London *Daily News*, described some of the more popular dishes:

Horse
'Eaten in the place of beef . . . a little sweeter . . . but in other respects much like it'

Cat
'Something between rabbit and squirrel, with a flavour all its own'

Donkey
'Delicious – in colour like mutton, firm and savoury'

Kittens
'Either smothered in onions or in a ragout they are excellent'

Rat
'Excellent – something between frog and rabbit'

Spaniel
'Something like lamb, but I felt like a cannibal'

'This siege will destroy many illusions,' Labouchère concluded, 'and amongst them the prejudice which has prevented many animals being used as food. I can most solemnly assert that I never wish to taste a better dinner than a joint of a donkey or a ragout of cat – *experto crede*.'

— — —

1872

A Plea to Be Kippered Jean-Henri Merle d'Aubigné, the Swiss pastor and historian of the Reformation, died on 21 October. Earlier in his life, when he had been staying in Scotland with Thomas Chalmers, leader of the Free Church of Scotland, he had been served kippers for breakfast. Intrigued, d'Aubigné asked what 'kipper' meant. He was told that it meant 'kept' or 'preserved'. Shortly after this, while leading the Chalmers family in their morning prayers, he requested that the Good Lord ensure that they be 'kept, preserved – and kippered'. (In fact, the word 'kipper' comes from Old English *cypera*, which in turn may derive from *coper*, 'copper', referring to the colour.)

1874

On the Dangers of Eating the Electorate In February Alfred Packer and five fellow prospectors set off across the wintry Rocky Mountains for the Colorado gold country, ignoring advice that they should wait until spring. On 16 April Packer arrived alone at the Los Pinos Indian Agency, near Gunnison. He claimed that he and his party had become completely lost and snowbound, and that one day, when he returned from foraging alone, he found that one of the party, Shannon Bell, had gone mad, killed the others with a hatchet, and had started to cook their flesh over a fire. Packer had then, he said, shot Bell in self-defence.

No one believed him, and at his subsequent trial the presiding judge, Melville B. Gerry, addressed the accused thus: 'Stand up, yah voracious man-eatin' sonofabitch, and receive your sentence. Thar were only seven Democrats in all of Hinsdale County and you ate five of them!' However, Packer escaped from jail, and was not recaptured for several years. In 1886 he was retried, found guilty of manslaughter and sentenced to 40 years. It was said that by the time of his death in 1907 he had become a vegetarian.

1876

Baked Alaska The name 'baked Alaska' was first used at Delmonico's Restaurant in New York, in honour of the cold northern territory acquired by the USA from Russia in 1867. The dessert, consisting of hot meringue surrounding frozen ice cream on a base of sponge cake, in fact originated in France, where it is known as *omelette à la norvégienne* ('omelette in the Norwegian fashion'), again alluding to the frozen north. The secret of the recipe is to place the ingredients in a very hot oven, so that the meringue cooks so quickly that the ice cream does not have time to melt.

In 1969 the Hungarian physicist Nicholas Kurti used a microwave oven to create a 'Reverse Baked Alaska', also known as a 'Frozen Florida', consisting of a frozen shell of meringue surrounding a hot filling.

1877

On Eating the Entrails of Small Birds In *Kettner's Book of the Table* Eneas Sweetland Dallas discussed the custom of cooking larks, doves and plovers without first gutting them, citing 'an ancient author' who claimed that 'larks eat only pebbles and sand, doves grains of juniper and scented herbs, and plovers feed on air'. This being the case, it is implied, there should be no unpleasantness involved in consuming their viscera.

1878

French Food Part Three: Gamey Grouse In his journal for 3 April Edmond de Goncourt recorded a housewarming celebration hosted by Emile Zola: 'Very tasty dinner, including some grouse whose scented flesh Daudet compared to an old courtesan's flesh marinated in a bidet.'

1879

Suprêmes de Volaille Jeannette The American ship the USS *Jeannette*, under the command of Lieutenant George W. DeLong, embarked from San Francisco and sailed for the Bering Strait between Alaska and Siberia. DeLong's idea was that once the ship reached the Arctic Ocean it would become frozen in the ice and so drift towards the North Pole – DeLong's intended destination. All was going according to plan until June 1881, when the pressure of the ice crushed the ship's hull, and the crew were forced to unload themselves and their equipment onto the ice. The following day the ship sank. The men divided into three parties, and began the long trek towards the Siberian mainland. Only one group survived. DeLong was not among those who safely returned, having starved to death near Yakutsk.

In June 1884, wreckage from the *Jeannette* was found near the southern tip of Greenland, suggesting to the Norwegian explorer Fridtjof Nansen that the Arctic ice was in constant motion from the coast of Siberia to the North American Arctic – a hypothesis that he successfully tested during his *Fram* expedition of 1893–6.

In 1892, prior to embarking on his expedition, Nansen had met the celebrated chef Auguste Escoffier while staying at the Savoy, and it was this meeting, together with the story of the *Jeannette*, that inspired Escoffier to create a new dish: Suprêmes de Volaille Jeannette. Somewhat gruesomely, this appropriately cold dish consists of poached escalopes of chicken sprinkled with tarragon and placed on a bed of foie gras and chicken jelly, the whole thing being encased in a sculpted block of ice. The dish was first served in June 1896 at the Savoy, to celebrate Nansen's rescue by a British expedition after he had become stranded on the remote Arctic archipelago of Franz Josef Land.

1880

Unpleasant Rhenish In *A Tramp Abroad*, Mark Twain tells us 'The Germans are exceedingly fond of Rhine wines;

they are put up in tall, slender bottles, and are considered a pleasant beverage. One tells them from vinegar by the label.'

Cannibalism by Proxy? The Italian explorer Luigi D'Albertis published *New Guinea: What I Did and What I Saw*, in which he describes how his two fellow-explorers were shocked when he told them they had just eaten a dish of crocodile. Their anxiety was that the crocodile might have previously eaten human flesh, thus making them guilty (after a fashion) of cannibalism. D'Albertis managed to put their minds at rest by insisting it had been a very small crocodile, and thus unlikely to have tasted of the forbidden fruit.

The New World relative of the crocodile, the alligator, is sometimes served up in a gumbo in the American Deep South. It is said to taste of fillet of flounder.

How to Eat a Pea The anonymous work by 'A Member of the Aristocracy', *Manners and Rules of Good Society*, advises that peas may only be eaten from the convex side of a fork. As a character says in W.S. Gilbert's *Ruddigore* (1887), 'The man . . . who eats peas with a knife, I look upon as a lost creature.'

1884

Tact Richard Trench, author of *Christ the Desire of All Nations*, *Notes on the Parables of Our Lord* and other learned works of piety, resigned as Archbishop of Dublin owing to poor health. Some time later he was invited to dine with his successor at his former home. Forgetting he was no longer the host, at the end of the meal he turned to his wife and declared, so that all the company could hear, 'My dear, I am afraid we must count this cook as one of your failures.'

Battenberg Cake In honour of the marriage of Queen Victoria's granddaughter Princess Victoria of Hesse and by Rhine to Prince Louis of Battenberg, a special cake was created, which in cross section has four squares, two pink and two yellow, in a check pattern. The squares represented the four Battenberg princes, Louis, Alexander, Henry and Francis Joseph. Prince Louis, the grandfather of Prince Philip, Duke of Edinburgh, moved after his marriage to Britain, where he pursued a career in the Royal Navy, rising in 1912 to the position of First Sea Lord. However, with the outbreak of the First World War, anti-German feeling forced his resignation, and to placate public opinion he anglicized his surname to Mountbatten. The name of Battenberg cake, however, remained unchanged – unlike

German toast, which became French toast (*see* 1346), or the hamburger, which became the Salisbury steak. The latter was named after the nutritionist Dr J.H. Salisbury (1823–1905), who during the American Civil War had recommended a diet of minced steak, onions and coffee for the troops.

— — —

Fried Cockchafer Grubs

The grubs of the cockchafer – a beetle hated by gardeners for the damage it causes their plants – make a tasty dish, according to Peter Lund Simmonds in his 1885 book, *The Animal Food Resources of Different Nations*:

A few years ago at the Café Custoza in Paris a great banquet was given for the special purpose of tasting the white grubs or cockchafer worms.

This insect, it appears, was first steeped in vinegar, which had the effect of making it disgorge the earth, etc., it had swallowed while still free.

Then it was carefully rolled up in a paste composed of flour, milk and eggs, placed in a pan, and fried to a bright golden colour.

The guests were able to take this crisp and dry worm

in their fingers. It cracked between their teeth. There were some fifty persons present, and the majority had a second helping.

1886

A New Luxury Item Heinz Baked Beans were launched in the United Kingdom at London's exclusive Fortnum & Mason store, where they were sold as a luxury item. At that time the baked beans were made in Canada, and were marketed as an exotic import. Until the Second World War, following the American tradition of 'pork and beans', the tins contained a piece of pork, but with the advent of rationing this was removed, and never returned (apart from a variant containing tiny sausages).

1888

Chinese Mixed Bits The Chinese dish known to the West as chop-suey had its first recorded mention in an English-language publication, namely the US journal *Current Literature*: 'A staple dish for the Chinese gourmand is chow chop svey [sic], a mixture of chickens' livers and gizzards, fungi, bamboo buds, pigs' tripe and bean sprouts stewed with spices.' There is a myth that the dish was created in California by a Chinese cook who, faced with a bare larder and some hungry and impatient white railway workers (or gold miners), rustled up some leftovers and fried them all together. The customers were not only mollified but delighted, and asked the cook what the dish was called. '*Chop suey,*' he reputedly replied, a phrase meaning 'odds and ends'. The supposed American origin of the dish was already widely believed by the turn of the century, the *Rochester Post-Express* (a newspaper from New York state) telling its readers in 1904 that 'One of the Chinese merchants of New York . . . explained that chop suey is really an American dish, not known in China, but believed by Americans to be the one great national dish of the Celestials.' In fact, the traditional Cantonese peasant dish of *shap sui*, meaning 'mixed bits', was brought to California in the 19th century by indentured labourers from southern China.

On Connoisseurship In *Le Rosier de Madame Husson*, Guy de Maupassant has one of his characters give this defence of gustatory discrimination:

> A man who cannot tell a crayfish from a lobster, or a herring, that admirable fish which comprises all the different flavours and essences of the sea, from a mackerel or a whiting, or a William pear from a Duchess, may be compared to a man who cannot distinguish Balzac from Eugène Sue, a Beethoven symphony from a military march by a regimental bandmaster, the Apollo Belvedere from the statue of Général de Blanmont.

1889

Drowning in Beer In *Twilight of the Idols*, the German philosopher Friedrich Nietzsche decried his country's submergence in beer:

This nation has arbitrarily stupefied itself for nearly a thousand years: nowhere have the two great European narcotics, alcohol and Christianity, been more wickedly misused . . . How much moody heaviness, lameness, humidity, and dressing-gown mood, how much beer is in German intelligence!

Pizza Margherita In June 1889 Queen Margherita of Italy was visiting Naples and, anxious to try the local speciality, she asked the pizza-maker Raffaele Esposito to visit the kitchens of the royal palace of Capodimonte. Esposito offered the queen three basic varieties: one with oil, one with whitebait, and one with tomatoes, to which Esposito added mozzarella and a little basil – red, white and green being the colours of the flag of the newly united Italy. The queen favoured this last variety, which was duly named in her honour, and her patronage helped to make pizza more acceptable across Italy. Prior to this, pizza was strongly associated with the poverty and filth of the Naples slums – as recently as 1886 Carlo Collodi, the Florentine creator of *The Adventures of Pinocchio*, had dismissed pizza as 'a patchwork of greasy filth'.

1891

A Play, a Riot and a Lobster Victorien Sardou's play *Thermidor* (named after one of the months in the French Revolutionary calendar) had its premiere at the Comédie-Française in Paris. The story, set during the Reign of Terror, tells how an actor saves the lives of many potential victims by infiltrating the Committee of Public Safety and destroying their files. Having heard that the play was critical of their hero Maximilien Robespierre, radical republicans crowded to the second performance and nearly caused a riot, prompting the intervention of the police and the clearing of the theatre. The play was subsequently banned by the government from all state-funded venues. However, *Thermidor* did give rise to a new dish, named in its honour by its creator, Tony Girod, the chef at the Café de Paris. This was the luxurious lobster Thermidor, which consists of lobster meat creamed with egg yolks and cognac, stuffed into a lobster shell and served with an oven-browned cheese crust.

On Water and Wine In the classic work on Italian cookery *Science in the Kitchen and the Art of Eating Well*, Pellegrino Artusi proffered the following advice:

> Some hygienists recommend that you drink water throughout lunch, keeping wine until the end. Do it

if you have the courage, but to me it seems like asking too much.

On this subject, G.K. Chesterton had this to say in his poem 'Wine and Water' (1914):

> And Noah he often said to his wife when he sat
>   down to dine,
> 'I don't care where the water goes if it doesn't get
>   into the wine.'

1892

The Birth of Shredded Wheat Henry D. Perky of Denver, Colorado, invented Shredded Wheat, a breakfast cereal that has since become iconic – as in the following anonymous rhyme, entitled 'Wine, Women and Wedding':

> The glances over cocktails
> That seemed to be so sweet
> Don't seem quite so amorous
> Over the Shredded Wheat.

There is a story told by the US comedian Fred Allen about the man who dreams he is eating Shredded Wheat and then wakes to find he has chewed away half the mattress. As it happens, Perky himself referred to his invention as 'my little whole wheat mattresses'.

1893

On the Status of Tomatoes The US Supreme Court, under Chief Justice Melville Weston Fuller, was asked to adjudicate on a crucial issue. After much deliberation, the court ruled that the tomato, although in botanical terms a fruit, was henceforth to be considered a vegetable.

1896

Why 57 Varieties? While riding in an elevated train in New York, H.J. Heinz was struck by a shoe shop sign declaring that it offered '21 styles'. He was thus inspired to come up with the slogan '57 varieties' for his own company – even though at that stage it was already selling many more lines. Heinz picked the number 57 largely because he liked the sound of it, although he chose 7 because of the 'psychological influence of that figure and its enduring significance to people of all ages'.

1897

Refried Beans Misnamed It is perhaps the fault of a Massachusetts newspaper, the *Lowell Sun*, that the beans the Mexicans call *frijoles refritos* are known in English as 'refried beans'. *Refrito* actually means 'well fried', but on 4

December a writer on the *Lowell Sun* – like many after him – assumed it meant 'refried'. The mistranslation has stuck.

— — —

Sole Véronique

In 1898, to celebrate the success of the London run of André Messager's new opera *Véronique*, the renowned chef Auguste Escoffier created a new dish, Sole Véronique, which involves a creamy white wine sauce and green grapes:

Roll up your fillets of sole, and place them in a lightly buttered frying pan.

Sprinkle in some chopped tarragon, and pour in a couple of glasses of dry white wine. Poach the fillets for three or four minutes, then remove from the pan onto a warm plate.

Reduce the poaching liquid to about one-third, stir in a cup or so of cream, and add the liquid to a roux, whisking as you go, to make a rich, creamy sauce.

Return the fillets to the frying pan, pour over the sauce and grill for two or three minutes, until golden-brown on top.

Serve garnished with peeled, halved and seeded green grapes.

An alternative account of the origin of the dish attributes the recipe to a Monsieur Malley, chef at the Paris Ritz, who dreamt up the idea and instructed one of his under-chefs to prepare it. As he did so, the young man heard that his wife had just given birth to a baby daughter. On learning that the girl was to be called Véronique, M. Malley named the dish in her honour.

1899

Oysters Rockefeller Jules Alciatore, the son of the founder of Antoine's restaurant in New Orleans, created a dish comprising oysters in a sauce of butter, watercress, spinach, shallots, celery, herbs, cayenne and Pernod. As the sauce was so rich, it was named after the richest man in America at the time, the oil magnate John D. Rockefeller.

On the Eating of Kiwis Although the kiwi, the flightless bird that has become a national symbol of New Zealand, is now completely protected, in former times it was hunted and eaten, as described by the explorer Charlie Douglas in his monograph on the birds of South Westland (*circa* 1899):

Just before they commence breeding they are very fat and good eating. Still I must confess it requires some considerable practice to get the acquired taste. They have an earthy flavour, which to many would be disagreeable. The best definition I ever heard about roast or boiled kiwi, was a man, remarking it tasted as he should imagine a piece of pork boiled in an old coffin would be like. The egg has slightly the same flavour . . .

The egg of the kiwi is the largest in relation to its body size of any bird in the world – and so, as Douglas informs us, 'One egg makes an excellent fritter, covering an ordinary frying pan.'

THE 20TH CENTURY

circa 1900

A One-Clawed Lobster The French *farceur* George Fey-
deau, while dining in an expensive restaurant, was angered
when he was presented with a one-clawed lobster. Raising
the matter with the maitre d', he was told that the lobsters
had been fighting in their tank. 'Then bring me the victor!'
he shouted.

1901

The Tongue Map Fallacy A German scientist, David
Hänig, published a paper entitled 'Zur Psychophysik des
Geschmackssinnes'. In translating this paper, the Harvard
psychologist Edwin G. Boring misleadingly gave the
impression that the 'fundamental' tastes of sweet, sour,
bitter and salt are each detected by different areas of the
tongue. This subsequently became received wisdom, and
the famous 'tongue map' was published in numerous text-
books. What the original paper actually showed was that
there were minute differences in *threshold* detection levels
across the tongue, but that all parts of the tongue are sensitive to all the tastes. In 1985 a fifth 'fundamental' taste,
umami – the 'meaty' taste of fermented fish sauce and
monosodium glutamate – was officially recognized by the

world of science, at the first Umami International Symposium in Hawaii.

1903

The Waiter's Revenge The Lone Star Saloon and Palm Garden Restaurant in Chicago's South State Street was closed down, its manager having been accused of lacing his customers' drinks with chloral hydrate – knock-out drops – so that he and his associates could pick their pockets. The manager's name was Mickey Finn. Hence if you are 'slipped a Mickey Finn', your drink has been spiked.

In 1918, some years after the closure of the Lone Star Saloon, 'Mickey Finn powder' featured in a notorious criminal case involving a large number of Chicago waiters who had been administering a powder containing antimony and potassium tartrate to customers whose tips they considered to be insufficiently generous. Those so poisoned suffered headaches, dizziness and vomiting, and some may even have died. Two people were arrested for manufacturing the powder, and two bartenders were charged with selling the powder at the headquarters of the waiters' union.

An Anti-Porkist William T. Hallett published his broadside, *Pernicious Pork; or, Astounding Revelations of the Evil Effects of Eating Swine Flesh*. In an introduction, a fellow anti-porkist who signed himself 'S.G.C.' launched straight into the matter in hand:

> Not since biblical times have we heard the clamorous warnings against the evils of eating swine flesh.
>
> The ancient Jews were a cleanly people in their food as well as their raiment, and, until these pages shall have been read, the unwholesomeness of pork can hardly be realized.
>
> It is small wonder the ancient race refused to eat of it, and it is astounding that civilization should permit its use. Why is it that no forceful will has arisen in denunciation and warning to stop this abhorrent practice?
>
> Are we not living in a progressive age? Are we not ascending the ladder of social improvement and scientific development? Yet a deadly evil such as this is permitted to flourish, with scarcely a dissenting voice to arrest the attention of the innocent and ignorant victims.

Hallett himself draws on the Bible and numerous case histories, including that of a young girl whose hands, 'through the eating of much pork, with accompanying gravies', had 'become so habitually festered or suppurated – especially about the fingers and the palms, with opened cracks in many of the creases – as to have become a most fearful affliction'. Then there were the children of another family known to the author, who, through the same cause, 'were affected with eruptive sores on nearly all parts of the person which suppurated, broke and scabbed, and as fast as they healed, and even before, others in adjacent places made their appearance'. There was also the case of the pork-gorging farmer who fathered four strapping sons, all of whom ended up drinking not just one, but two glasses of whisky at the end of their day's labour: 'It is enough to state that a lifelong habit of indulgence in polluting food by the sire, manifested its evil effects later in the sons, which was a decidedly inbred appetite of spirituous liquors.'

— ～ —

Scripture Cake

In the 1903 edition of *Practical Cookery*, Amy Atkinson and Grace Holroyd gave the following recipe for 'Scripture Cake'. The texts of the relevant verses have been inserted for the benefit of the ungodly.

4½ cups of I Kings 4:22
'And Solomon's provision for one day was thirty measures of fine flour . . .'

1½ cups of Judges 5:25
'. . . she brought forth butter in a lordly dish.'

2 cups of Jeremiah 6:20
'To what purpose cometh there to me . . . the sweet
cane from a far country? . . .'

2 cups of I Samuel 25:18
'Then Abigail made haste, and took . . . an hundred
clusters of raisins . . .'

2 cups of Nahum 3:12
'All thy strongholds shall be like fig trees with the first ripe
figs: if they be shaken, they shall even fall into the mouth
of the eater.'

1 cup of Numbers 17:8
'. . . and, behold, the rod of Aaron . . . bloomed
blossoms, and yielded almonds.'

2 tablespoonfuls I Samuel 14:25
'And all they of the land came to a wood; and there
was honey upon the ground.'

Season to taste II Chronicles 9:9
'And she gave the king . . . of spices great abundance
. . . neither was there any such spice as the queen of
Sheba gave king Solomon.'

6 cups Jeremiah 17:11
'As the partridge sitteth on eggs, and hatcheth them not . . .'

1 pinch Leviticus 2:13
'. . . with all thine offerings thou shalt offer salt.'

1 cup of Judges 4:19 last clause.
'And she opened a bottle of milk, and gave him drink . . .'

3 teaspoonfuls Amos 4:5
'And offer a sacrifice of thanksgiving with leaven . . .'

Follow Solomon's prescription for the making of a good boy and you will have a good cake, see Proverbs 23:14

'Thou shalt beat him with the rod, and shalt deliver his soul from hell.'

1904

The First Ice Cream Cones Although there are several conflicting accounts as to the invention of the first edible ice cream cone, the most charming version attributes it to Ernest A. Hamwi, an American of Syrian descent, who at the World's Fair in St Louis in 1904 helped out a neighbouring stallholder who had run out of dishes for his ice cream by rolling up his own Persian-style pastry, known as *ʒalabia*, into cones, in which scoops of ice cream were served to numerous appreciative customers.

1905

The First Popsicle One winter evening in San Francisco an 11-year-old called Frank Epperson left a glass containing a mixture of water and powdered flavouring, together with a stir stick, on the porch of his parents' house. That night temperatures in northern California plummeted, and in the morning young Frank found he had created an ice lolly. In 1923 he started selling his invention – which, in honour of himself, he called the Epsicle – and the following year applied for a patent. At his children's insistence he renamed it the Popsicle – a trademark now held by Unilever.

A Prediction In his book *A Hundred Years Hence*, T. Baron Russell made the following prophecy:

> Such a wasteful food as animal flesh cannot survive: and even apart from the moral necessity which will compel mankind, for its own preservation, to abandon the use of alcohol, the direct and indirect wastefulness of alcohol will make it impossible for beverages containing it to be tolerated.

On the Uses of Cotton-Wool Sandwiches In *Meals Medicinal*, W.T. Fernie describes the case of a patient 'who accidentally swallowed his false teeth through being struck in the face by a wave whilst swimming in the open sea':

He was treated with Sandwiches containing a thin layer of cotton-wool in each, between the slices of bread and butter; and after a week, when a mild laxative was given, the dental structure, being now enrolled in cotton-wool, was passed without difficulty amongst the excrement.

1906

Some Devil's Definitions Ambrose Bierce supplied the following definition in his *Devil's Dictionary*:

MACARONI, *n.* An Italian food made in the form of a slender, hollow tube. It consists of two parts – the tubing and the hole, the latter being the part that digests.

In the 1911 *Enlarged Devil's Dictionary*, we find the following definitions:

CUSTARD, *n.* A detestable substance produced by a malevolent conspiracy of the hen, the cow and the cook.

RHUBARB, *n.* Vegetable essence of stomach ache.

Poularde Sainte Alliance:
A Dish Fit For a King

In his *Guide to Modern Cookery* (1907) the renowned French chef and restaurateur Auguste Escoffier offered recipes of great complexity and lavishness, earning him the sobriquet 'king of chefs and chef of kings'. As the following instructions attest, the author was also deeply concerned with the manner in which his dishes should be served to the diners.

Escoffier first describes how the *poularde* (pullet or young hen) should be laid in a casserole on a layer of *matignon* (finely minced carrot, onion, celery heart, raw lean ham, thyme and bay leaf, all stewed in butter). Then melted butter is poured over the chicken and it is cooked in a low oven, with more melted butter poured on at frequent intervals until the meat is tender. The *poularde* is then removed and clear, well-seasoned veal stock boiled up with the *matignon*, which is then strained to produce a sauce for the dish. Meanwhile, ten fine truffles are heated in butter and Madeira. And then the show really begins . . .

When the pullet is ready, quickly cook as many ortolans [buntings or other small birds], and toss in butter as

278

many collops of foie gras as there are diners, and send them to the table at the same time as the pullet, together with the latter's *poëling*-liquor, strained and in a sauce-boat.

The waiter in charge should be ready for it with three assistants at hand, and he should have a very hot chafer on the side-board. The moment it arrives he quickly removes the *suprêmes* [breast fillets], cuts them into slices, and sets each one of these upon a collop of foie gras, which assistant No. 1 has placed ready on a plate, together with one of the truffles inserted into the pullet at the start.

Assistant No. 2, to whom the plate is handed forthwith, adds an ortolan and a little juice, and then assistant No. 3 straightaway places the plate before the diner.

The pullet is thus served very quickly, and in such wise as to render it a dish of very exceptional gastronomical quality.

- - -

1909

A Love of Music and Food Part Three: A Very Hungry Contralto The Austrian (later American) contralto Ernestine Schumann-Heink created the role of Clytemnestra in Richard Strauss's opera *Elektra*. Neither

Schumann-Heink nor Strauss had a particularly high opinion of the other's art, and during rehearsals Strauss reputedly told the orchestra, 'Play louder, I can still hear Madame Schumann-Heink singing!' For her part, Schumann-Heink was famously fond of her food. There is a story that one evening the Italian tenor Enrico Caruso came across her sitting alone at a restaurant in front of an enormous steak. 'You are surely not going to eat that alone, Ernestine?' Caruso inquired. 'No,' she replied. 'Mit potatoes.'

The conjunction of appetite and fine singing did not go unnoticed by the conductor Sir Thomas Beecham. Once, when asked why he always selected such ample ladies to sing the leading roles in his opera productions instead of their more sylph-like colleagues, he replied, 'Unfortunately, those sopranos who sing like birds eat like horses – and vice versa.'

A Proustian Moment Having dabbled in writing since his youth, Marcel Proust had no great faith in his own abilities until he experienced a gustatory epiphany, as he describes in *Swann's Way* (1913), the first volume of his great novel. The moment of enlightenment came when he tasted a madeleine – a small sponge cake in the shape of a scallop shell and flavoured with lemon zest:

And suddenly the memory revealed itself. The taste was that of the little piece of madeleine which on Sunday mornings at Combray . . . my aunt Léonie used to give me, dipping it first in her own cup of tea or tisane.

The experience provided Proust with a gateway into the world of his own past, which he went on to explore in great depth throughout the seven-volume *À la recherche du temps perdu* ('In Search of Lost Time' or 'Remembrance of Things Past').

The madeleine itself may have been named after an 18th-century French pastry cook called Madeleine Paulmier, although doubts have been cast as to whether such a person ever existed. Alternatively, the scallop shape suggests the symbol of the Christian pilgrim, so the name may be a reference to Mary Magdalene, the prostitute who became one of the first followers of Jesus.

1911

All for a Milk Pudding Sledmere House, the Yorkshire home of Sir Tatton Sykes, was reduced to a shell by a catastrophic conflagration. Sir Tatton had been too preoccupied with finishing one of his favourite milk puddings to take the appropriate action when the fire was first brought to his notice.

Squid: Useful for Deluding Hunger on a Desert Island In his travel book *Siren Land*, the British writer Norman Douglas, who made his home in Italy, describes squid as:

> ... an animated ink-bag of perverse leanings, which swims backwards because all other creatures go forwards and whose indiarubber flesh might be useful for deluding hunger on desert islands, since, like American gum, you can chew it for months, but never get it down.

Incidentally, Douglas's last words were said to be, 'Get these f***ing nuns away from me.'

1913

Flinging the First Custard Pie It is thought that it was the American comic actor Mabel Normand who first threw a custard pie on film, and that her target was probably Fatty Arbuckle. Arbuckle himself became a master of the technique, and audiences wondered at his ability to throw two custard pies simultaneously in opposite directions. Soon specialist suppliers were developing pies with robust bases and hyper-adherent fillings specifically for hurling

on-screen, and Hollywood directors were staging scenes involving the throwing of perhaps as many as a thousand pies.

1914

Waste Not Want Not As a subject of the Austro-Hungarian Empire and thus an enemy alien, the Polish anthropologist Bronisław Malinowski, who was working in Papua at the outbreak of the First World War, was faced with a choice by the Australian colonial authorities: internment, or exile to the Trobriand Islands off the northeast coast of Papua. He chose the latter, and it was while on the Trobriand Islands that Malinowski did some of his most important work. He later recalled:

I once talked to an old cannibal who, hearing of the Great War raging in Europe, was most curious to know how we Europeans managed to eat such huge quantities of human flesh. When I told him the Europeans did not eat their slain foes he looked at me with shocked horror and asked what sort of barbarians we were, to kill without any real object.

1919

The Rise of the All-Food Cocktail The USA introduced Prohibition, banning the manufacture and sale of alcoholic beverages. In a spirit of rebellion, the country's restaurants titillated their clients with a hint of the forbidden by offering them glasses of what was called 'fruit cocktail', which became immensely popular – as did the similarly innocuous 'shrimp cocktail'.

Another gastronomic consequence of Prohibition was the invention of Caesar salad. This was named after the Italian American restaurateur Caesar Cardini (1896–1956), who with the advent of Prohibition moved his operation just over the Mexican border so he could offer the American diners who came flooding to his restaurant anything to drink that they fancied. One Fourth of July he was so overwhelmed with guests that he almost ran out of ingredients, and to feed the hungry diners he scrambled together whatever he could find in the store cupboard: lettuce, parmesan, croutons, eggs, olive oil, lemon juice, black pepper and Worcestershire sauce. A legend was born.

As it turned out, banning alcohol in the USA proved unenforceable, and had little effect on consumption. Prohibition was ended in 1933.

1921

Food Fads of the Famous After taking a summer job picking string beans for a dollar per 12-hour day, future President Richard Nixon acquired a life-long revulsion for the vegetable.

1922

A Crucial Distinction The following exchange occurs in James Joyce's *Ulysses*: 'When I makes tea I makes tea, as old mother Grogan said. And when I makes water I makes water . . . Begob, ma'am, says Mrs Cahill, God send you don't make them in the one pot.'

The Fascist Diet Mussolini's Blackshirts took power in Italy, and attempted to impose a Spartan manliness on the nation's eating habits. The English might be a 'five-meals-a-day people' and America a 'beefsteak civilization', but

Italians should aspire to transcend their obsession with 'being fed and fattened'. Il Duce himself insisted that no one should spend more than ten minutes a day at table, and his hagiographers recounted how he would take nothing more than milk for breakfast and dinner, with a light lunch of meat, fish or an omelette, accompanied by boiled vegetables. In fact, the dictator's diet was dictated not so much by ideology as by the gastro-duodenal ulcer from which he suffered for much of his adult life.

1924

British Food Part Four: Bleakness and Taciturnity In his *Letters from England*, the Czech writer Karel Čapek wrote:

> The average cooking in the average hotel for the average Englishman explains to a large extent the English bleakness and taciturnity. Nobody can beam and warble while chewing pressed beef smeared with diabolical mustard. Nobody can exult aloud while ungluing from his teeth a quivering tapioca pudding.

circa 1925

Will Not Constipate In the mid-1920s, during a health craze in America, one enterprising manufacturer launched the 'Vegetable Sandwich', which consisted of dehydrated celery, peas, carrots and cabbage, coated in chocolate. On the wrapper it was unambiguously stated: 'Will Not Constipate'.

- - -

Chrysanthemum Salad

In *The Gentle Art of Cookery* (1925), the authors Mrs C.F. Leyel and Miss Olga Hartley included a chapter on flower recipes, such as cowslip pudding, ice cream of roses, and eggs cooked with marigolds. Here is their recipe for chrysanthemum salad:

Clean and wash in water about twenty chrysanthemum flowers picked from the stalks. Blanch them in acidulated and salted water; drain them and dry them in a cloth.

Mix them well into a salad composed of potatoes, artichoke bottom, shrimps' tails, and capers in vinegar.

Arrange this in a salad bowl, and decorate it with beetroot and hard-boiled egg. A pinch of saffron may be added to this salad for seasoning.

The dark yellow chrysanthemums are best. In Yokohama the flowers already prepared are sold in the greengrocers' shops.

- - -

1926

Table Manners of the Stars The film star and sex symbol Rudolph Valentino died on 23 August from the complications of appendicitis and gastric ulcers. The latter may have owed something to his eating habits. One evening, while dining with the writer Elinor Glyn and the producer Jesse L. Lasky, Valentino is said to have consumed five courses, belched constantly, guzzled up his companions' leftovers, slurped gravy from his plate, and picked his nose with a spoon. On another occasion, while dining in the Mayfair Hotel, London, he apparently dispensed with the cutlery and ate everything (including the custard) with his fingers. He then blew his nose on his table napkin, stood up and broke wind, declaring 'Better out than in!'

1927

Great Fat Maggoty Things In *Across Arctic America*, the Danish explorer and ethnographer Knud Rasmussen describes eating a meal of caribou with a group of Inuit during the course of his great transcontinental journey of 1921–4:

> Then came dessert; but this was literally more than we could swallow. It consisted of the larvae of the

caribou fly, great fat maggoty things served up raw just as they had been picked out from the skin of the beasts when shot. They lay squirming on a platter like a tin of huge gentles [maggots used as fishing bait], and gave a nasty little crunch under the teeth, like crushing a black-beetle.

His host Ingjugarjuk, noting his discomfort, told him no one would be offended if he did not eat the larvae. 'We all,' Ingjugarjuk reassured him, 'have our different customs.'

1929

Spanish Wine: Sulphurous Urination In a letter to Rhys Davis from Parma on Majorca, D.H. Lawrence wrote: 'The Spanish wine, my God, it is foul, catpiss is champagne compared, this is the sulphurous urination of some aged horse.'

1930

Hoover-Hog As unemployment soared at the onset of the Great Depression, Texans reduced in circumstances turned for sustenance to the creature known as the 'poor man's pig' – the armadillo. Just as the shanty towns that grew up across the USA became known as 'Hoover-villes', after the president under whose watch the Depression hit, so armadillos were dubbed 'Hoover-hogs'.

Futurist Food On 28 December, the Italian poet and editor Filippo Tommaso Marinetti, founder of the proto-Fascist art movement called Futurism, launched his 'Manifesto of Futurist Cooking' in the Turin newspaper *Gazzetta del Popolo*. The most controversial of the demands of the manifesto was the abolition of pasta, which Marinetti blamed for scepticism, lassitude, pessimism, irony and even

pacifism. Although the medical profession was inclined to agree that too much pasta made for obesity, many Italians were outraged, and the mayor of Naples, the spiritual home of pasta, told a reporter that 'the angels in heaven eat nothing but *vermicelli al pomodoro*'. Marinetti retorted that this only went to show what a boring place heaven is.

Marinetti also demanded the abolition of the knife and fork, and the creation of sculpted foods whose appeal would be to the eye rather than the palate. Futurist meals would be eaten in a mock-up of the interior of an aeroplane, complete with vibrations from mock engines, while ultraviolet lamps would activate the vitamins in the food. In his *Futurist Cookbook* Marinetti also describes a 'Tactile Dinner', during which diners wear pyjamas of different materials, such as sponge, cork, sandpaper or felt, and feed on caramel balls with surprise fillings, such as raw meat, chocolate, pepper, banana and garlic. To experience a dish of raw and cooked vegetables, they must bury their faces in the plate to feel the textures of the different greens. Then, when they lift their heads to chew, waiters spray them with perfume.

A Menu for the Holy Palate

In the spirit of Marinetti's *Manifesto of Futurist Cooking* (*see* 1930), a new restaurant opened in Turin in 1931. This was the Taverna del Santopalato ('Tavern of the Holy Palate'), a 'pulsating aluminium structure' that listed on its menu dishes such as:

Intuitive Antipasto
An orange stuffed with salami, butter, mushrooms in vinegar, anchovies and raw chillies

Equator + North Pole
An 'equatorial sea' of raw egg yolks out of which rises a conical island of meringue, topped by truffles cut into the shapes of aeroplanes

Ultravirile
A dish only for women, and containing cock's combs and fried testicle

Aroused Pig
A peeled salami rising vertically from a sauce of espresso coffee and eau de cologne

---

1933

Penguin Eggs The Vicomte de Mauduit published *The Vicomte in the Kitchen*, which included the following observations on penguin eggs: 'greenish white . . . about the size of a turkey's, should be eaten hard-boiled, cold with a salad. To hard-boil them takes about three-quarters of an hour; when shelled, the whites appear like pale green jelly . . . they are as delicious to the taste as they are attractive to the eye.' Another of his tips was to cook mussels with a silver sixpence. If the sixpence turns black, the mussels should be thrown in the bin.

Georges de Mauduit de Kervern, Vicomte de Mauduit, was born in 1893, the great-grandson of one of Napoleon's generals, who went into exile with the emperor on St Helena. The vicomte himself was a military pilot in the First World War, then made his home in England and published four books on cookery, the last being *They Can't Ration These* (1940), commending the joys of such freely available wild foods as squirrel, hedgehog, rook, sparrow, starling, frog, nettles, pine-cone kernels and samphire. The vicomte disappeared at the Fall of France. He probably died in Germany, having been captured by the Nazis.

High Tea Par Excellence

The British tradition of high tea was never more thoroughly observed than in Aberdeen, as described by Lewis Grassic Gibbon in *Scottish Scene* (1934):

Tea is drunk with the meal, and the order of it is this:

First, one eats a plateful of sausage and eggs and

mashed potatoes; then a second plateful to keep down the first.

Eating, one assists the second plateful to its final home by mouthfuls of oatcake spread with butter.

Then you eat oatcake with cheese.

Then there are scones.

Then cookies.

Then it is really time to begin on tea – tea and bread and butter and crumpets and toasted rolls and cakes.

Then some Dundee cake.

Then, about half past seven, someone shakes you out of the coma into which you have fallen and asks you persuasively if you wouldn't like another cup of tea and just *one* more egg and sausage.

― ― ―

1934

Culinary Disasters in the Antarctic Admiral Richard Byrd, the pioneer aviator and polar explorer, spent five winter months alone in the Antarctic, operating a meteorological station. Although a man of great resources and daring, he was clearly a disaster in the kitchen, describing in his book *Alone* how his jelly bounced like a rubber ball, how he had to scrape his flapjacks from the pan with a chisel, and how his *filet mignon* ended up 'darkened to the colour of an old cavalry boot'. His greatest failure, however, was his attempt to make corn-meal porridge:

Into a boiler I dumped what seemed a moderate quantity of meal, added a little water, and stood it on the stove to boil. That simple formula gave birth to a Hydra-headed monster. The stuff began to swell and dry up, swell and dry up, with fearful sucking noises. All innocently I added water, more water and still more water. Whereupon the boiler erupted like Vesuvius. All the pots and pans within reach couldn't begin to contain the corn meal that overflowed. It oozed over the stove. It spattered the ceiling. It covered me from head to foot. If I hadn't acted resolutely, I might have been drowned in corn meal. Seizing the container in my mitted hands, I rushed it to the door and hurled it far into the food tunnel. There it continued to give off deadly golden lava until the cold finally stilled the crater.

1935

British Food Part Five: How Not to Cook Cabbage In *Wine and Food*, Vyvyan Holland (the son of Oscar Wilde) opined that 'Nearly every woman in England is competent to write an authoritative article on how not to cook cabbage.' Fifteen years later, the *Daily Mirror* correspondent Cassandra (William Connor) waxed effusive on the subject:

> Boiled cabbage *à l'Anglaise* is something compared with which steamed coarse newsprint bought from bankrupt Finnish salvage dealers and heated over smoky oil stoves is an exquisite delicacy. Boiled British cabbage is something lower than ex-Army blankets stolen by dispossessed Goanese doss-house-keepers who used them to cover busted-down hen houses in the slum district of Karachi.

1937

The Birth of Spam Hormel Foods of the USA launched Spam (trademarked as SPAM), the tinned meat product consisting of chopped pork shoulder, ham, salt, water, modified potato starch and sodium nitrite. During the Second World War, Spam played a key part in the war effort, becoming a staple in the rations of Allied forces: between them, British and Red Army troops accounted for some 15 million tins every week. GIs also had their fill, variously describing the product as 'ham that didn't pass its physical' or 'meatloaf without basic training'. Spam has continued to be particularly highly regarded in some of the Pacific Islands where US forces were active: it is used, for example, in the traditional Okinawan dish of chanpuru, while in the 50th State it is sometimes referred to as 'Hawaiian steak'.

Much of the Spam sold in North America is manufactured in Hormel's home town of Austin, Minnesota (known as 'Spam Town USA'). The city not only has a Spam Museum and an annual Spam Jam carnival held on the Fourth of July, but also a restaurant with a menu devoted exclusively to Spam.

As a tongue-in-cheek tribute, for some 30 years the city of Austin, Texas held an annual festival around April Fool's Day formally known as the Pandemonious Potted Pork Festival, but more familiarly known as Spamerama, in which, in a mass cook-off, hundreds of contestants competed to come up with the most innovative Spam dishes, from Spam ice cream and guacaspamole, to spamalama ding dong, a concoction of Spam, whipped cream and chocolate. Various Spam-based sporting events are also held. Generally speaking, however, Spam has a reputation as 'poor people's food', and in Scotland the term 'Spam Valley' is applied to any area where the affluent appearance of the housing belies the reality of the poverty behind the doors.

The End of the Artichoke King On 21 December Fiorello La Guardia, mayor of New York, banned the sale, display or possession of globe artichokes in the city. It was a move to break the last vestige of power of the Mafia leader Ciro Terranova, known as 'the Artichoke King', who had risen to power and wealth in the early years of the century by buying artichokes in California and selling them in New York at a vast profit. Terranova, a key player in the Morello crime family, had already acquired such a violent reputation that New York greengrocers were only too willing to pay the inflated prices he charged. However, by the 1930s Terranova's star was in decline, and following La Guardia's action he was arrested on charges of vagrancy every time he attempted to re-enter the city. He died following a stroke in February 1938, at the age of 49.

Unrelatedly, the first Artichoke Queen, crowned in 1948 at the Artichoke Festival held in Castroville, California, was a certain Norma Jean Baker – later better known as Marilyn Monroe.

1940

An Advocate for the Consumption of Grass-Mowings On 2 May *The Times* published the following letter from a J.R.B. Branson, eager to contribute his ideas to the war effort:

Sir, In view of the publicity you have accorded to Mrs Barrow's letter, I hope that you will spare me space to say, as an advocate for the consumption of grass-mowings, that I have eaten them regularly for over three years, and off many lawns. The sample I am eating at present comes off a golf green on Mitcham Common. I have never suffered from urticaria or any of the symptoms Mrs Barrow mentions. Nor did any of the many of my horses to which I have fed grass-mowings, freshly cut and cleaned from stones, &c. For my own consumption I also wash them well.

More mainstream was the advice to extract the maximum nutritional value from the available food, as in the following frequently broadcast exhortation:

> Those who have the will to win
> Cook potatoes in their skin
> Knowing that the sight of peelings
> Deeply hurts Lord Woolton's feelings.

(Lord Woolton was Britain's wartime minister of food.)

The Honour of France Defended: Part One In June, one of Paris's top restaurants, La Tour D'Argent (said to have been founded in 1582), sought to protect its celebrated wine cellar from thirsty German soldiers occupying the French capital by walling up the best bottles. The wine cellar stills commands considerable respect, with its 450,000 bottles being valued at 25 million euros in 2009, while the restaurant's 400-page wine list offers some 15,000 different wines to diners.

The Honour of France Defended: Part Two In response to the pro-German government of Marshal Pétain establishing its seat in the spa town of Vichy, French chefs abroad came up with what they felt was a more patriotic name for the cold summer soup known as *vichyssoise*: they called it *crème gauloise*. The new name didn't catch on.

A Love of Music and Food Part Four: La Tetrazzini The Italian soprano Luisa Tetrazzini died on 28 April. She was well known for her love of food, and once declared in her maturity, 'I may be old, I may be fat, but I am still Tetrazzini.' There is a story that one day, prior to singing Violetta in *La Traviata*, she went out for a hearty lunch with Enrico Caruso. Some hours later, on stage, when it fell to the tenor John McCormack, playing Alfredo, to lift the dying Violetta in his arms, he found it almost impossible. He later said that it felt as though he were fondling a pair of automobile tyres – for Tetrazzini had eaten so much at lunch that she had removed her corsets. McCormack's discomfiture set off Tetrazzini in a fit of the giggles, picked up by McCormack – much to the astonishment of the audience.

The American dish Tetrazzini – diced chicken or seafood, mushrooms and almonds in a butter, cream, wine and parmesan sauce, served with pasta – is named in her honour. It is thought to have been invented around 1910 by Ernest Arbogast, chef at San Francisco's Palace Hotel, where Tetrazzini was long resident.

Mock Fish

Food shortages and rationing in Britain during the Second World War inspired considerable ingenuity among the country's cookery writers. The following recipe comes from Ambrose Heath's *More Kitchen Front Recipes*, published in 1941:

Bring half a pint of milk to the boil, and when it is boiling, shower in two ounces of ground rice, and add a teaspoonful of chopped onion or leek, a piece of margarine the size of a small walnut, and a seasoning of anchovy essence.

Let this simmer gently for twenty minutes, then take the pan off the fire, and stir in a well-beaten egg.

Mix well together, and then spread the mixture out in a
flat dish: it should be about half an inch thick.

When it is cold, cut it into pieces the size and
shape of fish fillets, brush these with milk, roll them in
breadcrumbs, and fry until golden-brown. Serve parsley
sauce with them.

— — —

1941

In the Name of Science Following the Nazi invasion of
the Soviet Union, the Agricultural Experimental Station at
Pavlovsk near St Petersburg (then known as Leningrad)
fell into German hands. Happily, by this stage Soviet scientists had managed to transfer the station's vast and
unique collection of tubers and seeds to a location within
Leningrad itself. The city then endured a terrible 872-day
siege at the hands of the Nazis.

During the first winter of the siege, the daily ration was
restricted to 125 grams (4.5 ounces) of bread, over half of
which consisted of sawdust. By the following winter, there
were no birds, rats or pets to be found anywhere in the
city. The starving citizens tried to make a milk substitute
out of the stewed entrails of cats, flavoured with cloves.
In the factories, workers were known to drink engine oil

and to eat the grease from the bearings in their machines. It was even rumoured that those who were buried in the evening would have been dug up before dawn.

The siege was not lifted until 1944, by which time a million civilians had died, the majority from hunger. Among the dead were the 12 scientists looking after the Pavlovsk collection, who preferred to starve to death rather than eat the seeds and tubers in their care, which they regarded as belonging to humanity as a whole.

The Pavlovsk Station continues to be of global importance, containing over 5000 varieties of seeds, especially of strawberries, blackcurrants, gooseberries, apples and cherries. However, in 2010 the station came under threat from a property developer who wanted to build private homes on the land. The developer argued that because the station contained a 'priceless collection', it had no monetary value and was therefore worthless. Joining in the Kafka-esque spirit of the affair, the Russian government's Federal Fund of Residential Real Estate Development (FFRRED) argued that as the collection was never registered, it did not officially exist.

Always Time for Champagne On the death of her husband Jacques Bollinger, head of the champagne house, Lilly Bollinger took over the business and proved, until her death in 1977, to be a tireless ambassador for the product. 'I drink it when I'm happy,' she would say, 'and when I'm sad. Sometimes I drink it when I'm alone. When I have company I consider it obligatory. I trifle with it when I'm not hungry and drink it when I am. Otherwise, I never touch it – unless I'm thirsty.' A century and a half before, the Emperor Napoleon had more succinctly declared, 'In victory you deserve it; in defeat you need it.'

A 40-Case War On hearing of the Japanese attack on Pearl Harbor, the hard-drinking American comedian W.C. Fields picked up the phone and ordered 40 cases of gin. John Barrymore, who was visiting Fields at the time, asked 'Are you sure that's going to be enough?' 'Sure,' replied Fields. 'I reckon it's going to be a short war.' On another occasion, asked why he never drank water, Fields replied, 'Fish f*** in it.'

1943

The Sitwell Egg Sir George Reresby Sitwell, 4th Baronet of Renishaw, died on 9 July. Sitwell shared the eccentricity but not the talents of his famous children Edith, Osbert and Sacheverell. He wrote profligately, producing such works as *Lepers' Squints*, *Acorns as an Article of Medieval Diet*, *The History of the Fork*, and a pamphlet pointing out the errors in Einstein's general theory of relativity. Among his inventions were a musical toothbrush, a small pistol for shooting wasps, and the 'Sitwell egg'. This last was an egg-free egg comprising a white made of rice, a yolk of smoked meat, and a shell of synthetic lime, which he proposed as a useful foodstuff for travellers. To this end, he turned up at the offices of Sir Gordon Selfridge, proprietor of the famous Oxford Street department store, unannounced but in silk hat and frock coat – a form of dress that appears to have gained him admittance, but no contract from Sir Gordon. In the hallway of his house at Renishaw Sir George had a notice erected, which read, 'I must ask anyone entering the house never to contradict me in any way, as it interferes with the functioning of the gastric juices and prevents my sleeping at night.'

1944

The Ducal Diet On 24 June, *The New Yorker* carried the following account of the eating habits of Duke Ellington, the celebrated band leader:

> Duke Ellington, who is always worrying about keeping his weight down, may announce that he intends to have nothing but Shredded Wheat and black tea. When his order arrives, he looks at it glumly, then bows his head and says grace. After he has finished

his snack, his expression of virtuous determination slowly dissolves into wistfulness as he watches Strayhorn [composer and arranger Billy Strayhorn, Ellington's long-term collaborator] eat a steak. Duke's resolution about not overeating frequently collapses at this point. When it does, he orders a steak, and after finishing it he engages in another moral struggle for about five minutes. Then he really begins to eat. He has another steak, smothered in onions, a double portion of fried potatoes, a salad, a bowl of sliced tomatoes, a giant lobster and melted butter, coffee, and an Ellington dessert – perhaps a combination of pie, cake, ice cream, custard, pastry, jello, fruit, and cheese. His appetite really whetted, he may order ham and eggs, a half-dozen pancakes, waffles and syrup, and some hot biscuits. Then, determined to get back on his diet, he will finish, as he began, with Shredded Wheat and black tea.

1945

The Accidental Invention of the Microwave An American engineer called Percy Spencer, while building radar sets for the Raytheon company, noticed one day that a chocolate bar in his pocket was starting to melt. He correctly attributed this to the microwaves radiating from the radar set he was working on – the heating effects of high-frequency electric fields having already been established in the 1930s. Spencer went on to use the radar set to cook popcorn, and then an egg, which exploded in the face of one of his colleagues. He then constructed a special metal box to concentrate the microwave energy, and that same year Raytheon patented the device. The first commercial microwave ovens went on sale in 1947. They were nearly 6 feet (1.8 metres) tall, weighed 750 pounds (340 kilograms), and sold for $5000.

Beaver Tail In *Cooking Wild Game* Frank G. Ashbrook and Edna N. Sater waxed lyrical about the tail and liver of the beaver:

> The tail is fatty tissue, rich and palatable when cooked, and was greatly relished by early trappers and explorers. The liver is large and almost as tender and sweet as that of chicken or goose. The body meat has rather a gamy flavour, but if properly cared for and cooked is excellent and was generally preferred by trappers to any other game, even in the early days when buffalo, elk and deer were abundant.

Apparently the Native Americans would smoke the body meat to eliminate the gaminess.

1946

A Way With Bills In *Reader's Digest* the burlesque entertainer Gypsy Rose Lee told the following story: 'I once had lunch with Groucho Marx, a big lunch with terrapin and pitchers of wine. When he got the bill, he studied it like a bank examiner, added it up three or four times, then sprinkled it with sugar and ate it.'

1948

On the Supremacy of US Cuisine The American restaurant critic Duncan Hines returned to the USA after a tour of Europe, declaring that American cooking was the best in the world. This astonishing conclusion may have been influenced by the fact that Europe was still recovering from the ravages of the Second World War, and many foodstuffs were still scarce or completely unavailable.

A contrary view is provided by André Simon, the French wine guru and gourmet, who visited the USA frequently in the 1930s, and wrote in *Food and Drink*, the journal he founded:

> The average American probably spends more than the average citizen of any other country in the world upon food and drink, but he certainly is less well-nourished than the ordinary peasant class in any part

of Europe. To say nothing of the little French bourgeois whose income is half that of a New York elevator boy, and yet feeds far better than a Chicago packing millionaire.

All I Want for Christmas A radio station in Washington DC phoned around various ambassadors in the city to ask what they would like for Christmas, and then broadcast the results the following week. The French ambassador opted for world peace, while the Soviet envoy asked for 'freedom for all people enslaved by imperialism'. 'It's very kind of you to ask,' replied the British ambassador, Sir Oliver Franks, unaware of what his counterparts were saying, 'I'd quite like a box of crystallized fruit.'

1949

In Praise of the Martini Cocktail In *Harper's Magazine*, the American historian Bernard De Voto wrote about America's favourite cocktail:

> You can no more keep a martini in the fridge than you can keep a kiss there. The proper union of gin and vermouth . . . is one of the happiest marriages on earth and one of the shortest lived.

H.L. Mencken called the martini 'the only American invention as perfect as the sonnet', while to E.B. White it was 'the elixir of quietude'. Others celebrated its potency, as in the following anonymous rhyme:

> 'I love a Martini,' said Mabel,
> 'I only have two at the most.
> After three I am under the table,
> After four, I am under the host.'

Over the years, the gin-to-vermouth ratio steadily increased so that by the height of the Cold War the Soviet leader Nikita Khrushchev was calling the martini America's 'most lethal weapon'.

1950

In the Pink The eccentric English composer, painter, writer and aesthete, Gerald Hugh Tyrwhitt-Wilson, 14th Baron Berners, died on 19 April. At his house in Faringdon, Oxfordshire he would entertain his guests with meals restricted to a particular colour. For example, if feeling pink, Berners would arrange a luncheon menu of beet soup, followed by lobsters, tomatoes and strawberries, while outside he would arrange for a flock of pigeons, especially dyed pink, to fly past the windows.

1951

Too Many Cheeses General Charles de Gaulle despaired of his native land, sighing, 'How can you govern a country which has 246 varieties of cheese?'

Honey Ants In his masterly *Insects as Human Food*, F.S. Bodenheimer gives a vivid description of a particular species of Australian ant in which some of the workers are modified so that their grossly enlarged abdomens become repositories for honey, apparently to 'provide for the needs of the colony during the barren season of the year, acting as living barrels, which can be tapped as required'. These honey ants are a great delicacy for the Aborigines:

> When a native wishes to partake of the honey, he grips one of the ants by the head, and placing the swollen abdomen between his lips he squeezes the contents into his mouth and swallows them. As regards the taste, the first reaction the palate receives is a distinct prick of formic acid, which is no doubt due to a secretion produced by the ant in self-defence. But this is both slight and momentary; and the instant the membrane bursts, it is followed by a delicious and rich flavour of pure honey.

1952

Cephalopod Compared to Celluloid Arthur Grimble published *A Pattern of Islands*, a memoir of his time as a district officer in the Gilbert Islands (now part of Kiribati) in the South Pacific. Among other things, the author tells us of the method the islanders used to catch octopus: the diver would plunge under the water and bite the creature right between the eyes until it died. Once caught, octopus must be beaten repeatedly on the ground to tenderize it. D.H. Lawrence complained that even after this treatment the cephalopod had 'the consistency of boiled celluloid' (*Sea and Sardinia*, 1921). For his part, Noël Coward confided: 'I have eaten octopus – or squid, I can never quite tell the difference – but never with wholehearted enjoyment on account of not caring for the taste of hot India rubber.'

1953

Bah Humbug: Turkey vs Goose On 24 December, the *Daily Mirror* columnist Cassandra (William Connor) had this to say of the millions of turkeys awaiting to be consumed the following day across Britain:

> What a shocking fraud the turkey is. In life preposterous, insulting – that foolish noise they make to

scare you away! In death – unpalatable. The turkey has practically no taste except a dry fibrous flavour reminiscent of a mixture of warmed-up plaster-of-Paris and horsehair. The texture is like wet sawdust and the whole vast feathered swindle has the piquancy of a boiled mattress.

Of course, in Dickens's day, it was goose not turkey that graced the Christmas table:

> There never was such a goose. Bob said he didn't believe there ever was such a goose cooked. Its tenderness and flavour, size and cheapness, were the themes of universal admiration. Eked out by apple-sauce and mashed potatoes, it was a sufficient dinner for the whole family; indeed, as Mrs Cratchit said with great delight (surveying one small atom of a bone upon the dish), they hadn't ate it all at last! Yet every one had had enough, and the youngest Cratchits in particular, were steeped in sage and onion to the eyebrows!
>
> Charles Dickens, *A Christmas Carol* (1843)

Not everybody had such a high opinion of the ability of a goose to feed the whole family:

The goose is a silly bird – too much for one to eat, and not enough for two.

> Charles H. Poole, *An Attempt towards a Glossary of the Archaic and Provincial Words of the County of Stafford* (1880)

1956

Matzoh Balls When dining at the parents of her new husband, Arthur Miller, Marilyn Monroe was offered matzoh balls. According to oral tradition, she replied, 'Isn't there another part of the matzoh you can eat?'

1957

Far Too Good for My Publisher The French writer, director, actor and producer Yves Mirande died on 20 March. Mirande was a man of prodigious appetites, according to A.J. Liebling's book *Between Meals* (1962):

In the restaurant on the Rue Saint-Augustin M. Mirande would dazzle his juniors, French and American, by dispatching a lunch of raw Bayonne ham and fresh figs, a hot sausage in crust, spindles of filleted pike in a rich rose sauce Nantua, a leg of lamb larded with anchovies, artichokes on a pedestal of foie gras, and four or five kinds of cheese, with a good bottle of Bordeaux and one of champagne, after which he would call for the Armagnac and remind Madame to have ready for dinner the larks and ortolans she had promised him, with a few langoustes and a turbot – and, of course, a fine civet [stew] made from the *marcassin*, or young wild boar, that the lover of the leading lady in his current production had sent up from his estate in the Sologne. 'And while I think of it,' I once heard him say, 'we haven't had any woodcock for days, or truffles baked in the ashes, and the cellar is becoming a disgrace – no more '34s and hardly any '37s. Last week, I had to offer my publisher a bottle that was far too good for him, simply because there was nothing between the insulting and the superlative.'

Mud as a Foodstuff Robert Beauchamp, director of the East African Fisheries Research Organization based in Jinja, Uganda, suggested that mud from the bottom of Lake Victoria could provide a valuable feed for pigs and poultry – and even for humans. He had analysed the mud, which showed high levels of nutrients, and declared that he and his family and friends found it a perfectly acceptable dish.

1962

Space Food When John Glenn became the first American to orbit the Earth on 20 February, aboard *Friendship 7*, he also became the first person to eat food in space: a tube of apple purée. Space food has to be carefully packaged and consumed. When John Young and Gus Grissom returned from the first two-man space flight aboard *Gemini 3* in March 1965, the former was severely reprimanded for smuggling on board a corned-beef sandwich, whose crumbs, in the zero-gravity conditions, could have interfered with the spacecraft's sensitive instruments. Young was doubly aggrieved, as it was Grissom who'd eaten the sandwich.

1963

Spanish Food: Never Up To Much Writing in the *Spectator* on 23 November, the English novelist Kingsley Amis had this to say about Spanish food:

> The meal was of course filthy. It began with glazed seafood and continued with ridiculously tough veal or something, the whole washed down with vile wine. Spanish food and drink were never up to much in my experience, but you used to be able to depend

on simplicities like tomatoes, onions, olives, oranges and the local red. Not now. The bread has gone too. The only things that are always all right are potatoes, tinned fruit, ice cream and sherry. And Coca Cola, I dare say.

1967

A Potato Dependency 'To deprive a Dane of his boiled potatoes,' wrote Nika Hazelton in *Danish Cooking*, 'would be as cruel as depriving a baby of its bottle.'

1970

You Can't Take It With You The wine merchant, gourmet and writer André Simon died on 5 September. He once said: 'A man dies too young if he leaves any wine in his cellar.' At the time of his death, Simon was 93, and all that remained in his cellar were two magnums of claret.

1976

British Food Part Six: Mangel-Wurzels and Suet In *National Lampoon*, Tony Hendra noted that:

From time immemorial, the English, saddled with a climate that produced nothing tastier than mangel-wurzels and suet, have been forced to import anything that would stay down for more than ten seconds.

He was no more flattering to the Danes in the kitchen department: 'Who else would have the sense of humor to stuff prunes and toecheese into lumps of wet dough and *serve it to you for breakfast?*'

French Food Part Four: Cheese That Smells Like People's Feet In his *National Lampoon* survey of 'Foreigners Around the World', P.J. O'Rourke spoke of the French as 'Utter cowards who force their own children to drink wine . . . sawed-off cissies who eat snails and slugs and cheese that smells like people's feet'. Regarding snails, O'Rourke's fellow American, Miss Piggy, told the readers of *Miss Piggy's Guide to Life* (1981), 'I find this a somewhat disturbing dish, but the sauce is divine. What I do is order escargots, and tell them to "hold" the snails.'

Fried Locusts, South African Style

Louis C. Leipoldt, in *Leipoldt's Cape Cookery* (1976), supplied the following recipe for fried locusts:

Nip off their wings, heads and legs, after you have

plunged them into boiling water mercifully to kill them.

What remains are the thorax and abdomen, which are the only parts that interest the epicure.

You dust them with a mixture of pepper and salt (to which for some absurd reason that I have never been able to understand, some people add a little powdered cinnamon) and shallow-fry them in fat till they are crisp and brown.

They taste not unlike whitebait that, somehow, have been stuffed with buttered toast.

~ ~ ~

1977

Southern Food Prior to her husband taking up office, Rosalynn Carter asked the White House chef whether he could prepare the kind of Southern dishes that she and Jimmy were used to back in Georgia. 'No problem, ma'am,' the chef replied. 'We've been serving that kind of food to the servants here for many years.'

circa 1980

The Cocktail Revival As Britain was hit by a plague of new cocktail bars, ushering in the Thatcher era, one disgruntled Glaswegian was heard to complain: 'Ah mind whin drink wi' bits o' food in it wiz called vomit.'

1981

If You're Going to America, Bring Your Own Food So wrote Fran Lebowitz in her 1981 book *Social Studies*. More than half a century earlier, the dancer Isadora Duncan had told an interviewer, 'I would rather live in Russia on black bread and vodka than in the United States at the best hotels. America knows nothing of food, love, or art.' The British broadcaster Robert Robinson dismissed the whole continent, saying merely that 'The national dish of America is menus.'

Continental Breakfasts That same year, Miss Piggy, in *Miss Piggy's Guide to Life*, advised that 'Continental breakfasts are very sparse, usually just a pot of coffee or tea and teensy roll that looks like a suitcase handle. My advice is to go right to lunch without pausing.' Regarding Chinese cuisine, Miss Piggy opined, 'You do not sew with a fork, and I see no reason why you should eat with knitting needles.'

Rocky Mountain Oysters

In 1982 the town of Clinton, Montana, held its first
Testicle Festival, an event at which visitors annually
consume over 2 tons of bull's testicles. One of the
favourite ways of serving these is as 'Rocky Mountain oysters', apparently long a favourite among
cowboys:

First castrate your male calf, and throw the testicles into
a bucket of water.

Then peel the testicles, wash them and slice them into
ovals.

Roll the ovals in a mixture of flour, cornmeal, beaten
eggs, salt and pepper, then deep fry.

Serve with a hot pepper sauce.

Other gastronomic euphemisms for testicles include
prairie oysters, barnyard jewels, cowboy caviar, fry,
swinging beef and Montana tendergroin. The French
call them *animelles*, while the Greeks include them
in the offal stew known as *kokoretsi*.

1984

British Food Part Seven: Pre-Eminence in the Matter of Tea Wilfrid Sheed contributed an article entitled 'Taking Pride in Prejudice' to *GQ* magazine, in which he opined:

> English cuisine is so generally threadbare that for years there has been a gentlemen's agreement in the civilized world to allow the Brits pre-eminence in the matter of tea – which, after all, comes down to little more than the ability to boil water.

Some years earlier, in *Marlene Dietrich's A B C* (1962), we read:

> The British have an umbilical cord which has never been cut and through which tea flows constantly. It is curious to watch them in times of sudden horror, tragedy or disaster. The pulse stops apparently, and nothing can be done, and no move made, until 'a nice cup of tea' is quickly made.

Even earlier, Hilaire Belloc had declared: 'If I had known there was no Latin word for tea, I would have let the vulgar stuff alone.'

The Monkey Brain Myth In the *Listener* magazine, the distinguished food writer Derek Cooper sought to expose as myth the rumour that certain wealthy Chinese in the Far East had a fondness for a particular food: the brains of monkeys, scooped out of their skulls while they were still alive. Supposedly, the unfortunate creatures were restrained in some kind of device placed in the centre of the table, while the diners ate their fill. In *The Oxford Companion to Food* (1999), another distinguished food writer, Alan Davidson, suggested that it might well have been Cooper himself who had started the rumour.

1985

The Sociology of Asparagus Bill Rathje, a professor at the University of Arizona, concluded from his analysis of discarded asparagus stalks in people's garbage, that 'the higher your income the higher up the stalk you cut off the tip'.

A Very Special Vintage At Christie's a bottle of 1787 Château Lafite was sold for £105,000. At that age the wine would have been quite undrinkable, but it was the first owner of the bottle that gave it such cachet. This was none other than Thomas Jefferson, one of the founding fathers and third president of the USA.

On the Dangers of Sweetness The Austrian wine industry was hit by a major scandal, when it emerged that millions of bottles of that year's vintage were 999 parts wine and 1 part diethylene glycol – antifreeze – which had been added to lend extra sweetness.

1990

Contra Broccoli President George Bush Snr denounced his least favourite vegetable at a news conference on 22 March:

> I do not like broccoli and I haven't liked it since I was a little kid and my mother made me eat it. And I'm President of the United States and I'm not going to eat any more broccoli. Now look, this is the last statement I'm going to have on broccoli. There are truckloads of broccoli at this very minute descending on Washington. My family is divided. For the broccoli vote out there: Barbara loves broccoli. She has tried to make me eat it. She eats it all the time herself. So she can go out and meet the caravan of broccoli that's coming in.

American broccoli growers were incensed, and dumped 10 tons of the stuff on the steps of the White House. 'Just wait till the country hears how I feel about cauliflower,' quipped the president. He proceeded to denounce carrots as 'orange broccoli'.

1992

Gum Ban Singapore banned the importation, sale and possession of chewing gum, following a number of occasions when gum discarded on train doors had brought about the complete breakdown of the city's Mass Transit System. Pressure from the USA resulted in a partial lifting of the ban in 2004, when the importation of 'therapeutic' sugar-free gum was permitted once more.

1993

The Sorry Fate of Chris P. Carrot Ten years after the event, *Rolling Stone* carried the following story:

> People for the Ethical Treatment of Animals [PETA] uses a menagerie of lovable animal mascots, and many have suffered abuse by the public. A September 1993 appearance at Douglas Elementary School in Des Moines, Iowa, turned ugly when PETA's vegetarian mascot, Chris P. Carrot, was attacked by a mob of meat-wielding children. The kids stuffed

beef jerky into Mr Carrot's costume, then chased him down the street. A shocked TV reporter grabbed one of the boys and said, 'You leave that carrot alone!' The other kids chanted, 'F--- PETA! We love meat!' and threw bologna at Mr Carrot's van as he sped away.

1995

Snail Porridge The innovative and almost entirely self-taught British chef Heston Blumenthal opened his restaurant, The Fat Duck, at Bray in Berkshire. It was not an auspicious start, as on the second day after opening the oven exploded, and Blumenthal was obliged to continue working with a bag of frozen peas clamped to his head. Despite such upsets, Blumenthal gained an enormous reputation (and three Michelin stars) for his whimsical-cum-scientific approach to the creation of new dishes, throwing away the rule book to come up with such creations as beetroot crumble, bacon-and-egg ice cream and snail porridge.

1996

Dining in Siberia In 'Raw Liver and More', a paper delivered to the Oxford Symposium on Food and Cookery,

Sharon Hudgins described a speciality of the Buryat people, who live around Lake Baikal in southern Siberia:

> Placed in front of me was the sheep's stomach, which had been filled with a mixture of fresh cow's milk, fresh sheep's blood, garlic and spring onions, tied up with the sheep's intestines, and boiled in the pot with the rest of the meat . . . Our hostess leaned over and sliced the top of the stomach. The contents had not been fully cooked and blood oozed onto my plate. She took a large spoon, scooped out some of the semi-coagulated mass, and handed a spoonful to me . . .

1998

Cicadas and Chardonnay The naturalist David George Gordon published his *Eat-a-Bug Cookbook*, trumpeting the delights of an insectivorous diet. Gordon pointed out that the US Food and Drug Administration permits 60 aphids to every 100 grams of frozen broccoli, up to 3 fruit-fly maggots in 200 grams of tomato juice, and 56 insect parts in a single peanut and jelly sandwich. He went on to provide a wealth of recipes for bees, ants, grasshoppers, crickets and locusts. As for cicadas, the nymphs (which taste of asparagus) make a good pizza topping, while the adults are crunchy and nutty, and best washed down with a glass of chardonnay.

In the USA, the simultaneous emergence of millions of adult cicadas every 13 or 17 years (depending on the species) prompts many cooks to dust down some traditional recipes. Some like to sautée their cicadas in butter and garlic, others to bake them into banana bread or rhubarb pie, while many prefer them simply dipped in chocolate as a snack. In 2011 (a 13-year-cycle year), one enterprising ice cream parlour in Missouri offered boiled bugs covered with brown sugar and milk chocolate, mixed into an ice cream base of brown sugar and butter. However, the local department of environmental health advised the parlour against the idea.

The Viennese Vegetable Orchestra In Vienna some enterprising young musicians, visual artists, writers and

other creatives formed the Vegetable Orchestra, which has become famous for its performances on instruments fashioned from fresh as well as dried plant material such as carrot, leek, celery root, artichoke, dried pumpkin and onion skin. As the orchestra's website says:

> The sounds produced by the vegetable instruments are amazingly multi-layered: transparent & crackling, shrill & massive, dark & hypnotic, funky & groovy – a heterogeneous multitude of acoustic gems and strange, unfamiliar sounds whose organic origin is not always immediately recognizable . . . There are no musical boundaries for the Vegetable Orchestra. The most diverse music styles fuse here – contemporary music, beat-oriented House tracks, experimental Electronic, Free Jazz, Noise, Dub, Clicks'n'Cuts – the musical scope of the ensemble expands consistently, and recently developed vegetable instruments and their inherent sounds often determine the direction.

At the end of each performance the instruments are turned into fresh vegetable soup, which is shared among the audience.

THE 21ST CENTURY

2000

Correcting an Image Problem As sales of prunes steadily declined through the 1990s – largely due to the image of the product as an old person's laxative – the Prune Board of California lobbied the Food and Drug Administration requesting permission to change the name. Eventually in 2000 the FDA relented, and prunes officially became known as 'dried plums'.

2001

Getting One's Priorities Right One of President George W. Bush's first actions on taking office was to add a new item to the menu at the White House: peanut butter and jelly sandwiches.

Britain's New National Dish In homage to the multicultural spirit of the age, Foreign Secretary Robin Cook declared that chicken tikka masala was Britain's new national dish. Critics immediately condemned the dish as a British invention, an example of the national tendency to take an authentic foreign dish and bastardize it to suit the unsophisticated taste of the average Briton. In the case of chicken tikka masala, it was said that it originated when a customer at an Indian restaurant complained that his chicken tikka was too dry. So the cook mixed up a tin of Campbell's tomato soup with some cream and spices, and poured it over the chicken. A legend was born.

To confuse the culinary/cultural pot still further, it should be pointed out that most 'Indian' restaurants in Britain are actually run by Bangladeshis. Furthermore, until the 1990s, most of these owners were relatives and neighbours from a small area around the city of Sylhet, in the northeastern corner of Bangladesh.

An Icelandic Delicacy In the *Sunday Telegraph* on 27 December the travel writer Jonathan Young described an experience he had once had in Iceland:

> 'First you urinate on the meat, then bury it for four months before digging it up and eating it raw,' explained Loftur, pushing a saucer of diced Greenland shark towards us. It sounds like a joke . . .
>
> 'No, really, it's a traditional Icelandic dish,' insisted Loftur, popping an off-grey cube into his mouth and gulping down a shot of *brennivin* (literally 'burnt wine'). 'Go on!'
>
> The sensation was not unpleasant – so long as I remembered not to breathe. If I did, ammonia of rotted shark gave my lungs a sound kicking and threatened to coax up yesterday's breakfast.

2003

The World's Priciest Salad Raymond Blanc, chef of Le Manoir Aux Quat' Saisons in Oxfordshire, presented the 'Florette Sea and Earth Salad' at a special event at the Hempel Hotel in London's Bayswater. In order of cost per portion, the creation contained the following ingredients:

Potato 10p

Red romano peppers 50p

Moulin Jean Marie Cornille olive oil 50p

Florette baby leaf salad 50p

Cornish crab £2

30-year-old balsamic vinegar £3

Cornish lobster £5

Kreel-caught langoustines £5

Truffle £5

Gold leaf £5

Beluga caviar £9

Almas golden caviar £600 (for 50 grams)

The truffles and caviar were presented in a basket handmade from courgettes, red peppers and potatoes, and decorated with gold leaf, and the total cost per serving was £635.60. Almas golden caviar was once reserved for the tsars of Russia, and sells at £12,000 per kilo.

The City That Refused to Become Veggieburg Animal-rights activists in Hamburg made the city an offer they thought it could not refuse: they said they would donate 10,000 euros to childcare groups if Hamburg changed its name to Veggieburg. 'I don't even want to look at nonsense like this,' said a spokesman for the city. 'But that doesn't mean we Hamburgers don't have a sense of humour.'

Hitlerian Tipple Causes Ruckus Something of a diplomatic incident occurred when the German justice minister demanded that the Italian government ban the sale of so-called Führerwein, some 30,000 bottles of which were being sold annually, mostly to German tourists. The labels had a picture of Hitler together with such Nazi slogans as '*Blut und Ehre*' and '*Ein Volk, ein Reich, ein Führer*'. The Italian winery of Alessandro Lunardelli had been producing Führerwein for some five years, alongside bottles celebrating Mussolini and Stalin.

2004

Welsh Scotch On St David's Day, the Welsh Whisky Company (aka *Y Cwmni Wisgi Cymreig*) launched its Penderyn single malt. The producers claim that whisky is also a Welsh tradition, where barley-based spirit was known as *gwirod*. Legend has it that the first *gwirod* was distilled on Bardsey Island (known as the 'Island of 20,000 Saints') in the 4th century AD by a man called Reaullt Hir. Several centuries later, in 1705, a commercial distillery opened in Dale, Pembrokeshire, and Evan Williams, a family-member of the owners, emigrated to the USA where he had a hand in founding the whiskey industry in Kentucky – leading some to claim that Jack Daniels has Welsh roots. The spread of the chapel-based temperance movement in Wales put an end to the Welsh distilling industry, the last still (at Frongoch, near Bala) closing in 1896.

Two Ways of Cooking a Badger

In their 2004 book *Les Cuisines oubliées*, Annie and Jean-Claude Molinier presented a collection of long-forgotten French rustic recipes, including beaver stew, roast hedgehog, squirrel in a pot and magpie baked in clay. There is even a recipe for fox – which must be skinned and left in a river for three days prior to cooking (and is still pretty unpleasant). As for badger, the best method is *blaireau au sang*:

First flambée the badger meat in Armagnac.

Then simmer it in white wine, with ginger, eggs and cream.

Finally, pour a glass of pig's blood into the dish
before serving.

In England in Anglo-Saxon times badgers were also
a delicacy, slowly smoked over a birch-wood fire. It
was best to catch your badger in the autumn, when
it had built up a thick layer of fat in preparation for
the winter.

— — —

2006

Dear Leader Guzzles Giant Bunnies, Allegedly Robert,
the largest rabbit in Germany, weighing in at 23 pounds 2
ounces (10.5 kilograms) and sporting ears 8 inches (20
centimetres) long, was invited, along with 11 of his dog-
sized fellows to North Korea, with the aim of setting up a
breeding farm to end the country's food shortages. Anxious
to help, Robert's breeder, 67-year-old Karl Szmolinsky,
offered the North Koreans a cut-price deal. Szmolinsky
had been expecting to visit North Korea to inspect the
breeding facility, but the North Koreans cancelled the trip
at short notice. Szmolinsky suspected the worst, believing
that Robert and his friends and relations were eaten by
Kim Jong Il, the 'Dear Leader' of North Korea, at his

birthday banquet in January 2007. The North Korean embassy in Berlin denied the suggestion.

2007

Death of Monsieur Mangetout On 25 June Michel Lotito, better known by his stage name 'Monsieur Mangetout' ('Mr Eat-Everything'), died of natural causes at the age of 57. He had made his name by consuming a variety of indigestible materials, such as metal, glass and rubber, and during his career had managed to eat several bicycles, televisions, shopping trolleys and even – over a period of two years – a Cessna 150 light aircraft. Doctors who examined him found that his stomach lining was twice as thick as that of

most people, which may partly explain why he suffered from no ill effects. Swallowing copious amounts of water and mineral oil also seems to have helped the nuts and bolts slip through his system.

2008

Wash Testicles Thoroughly The Serbian chef Ljubomir Erovic published *The Testicle Cookbook*. In it, the recipe for testicle pie includes the following instruction: 'Wash testicles thoroughly and boil them for 30 to 45 minutes. Once softened, mince them in a mincer.'

2009

The Dangers of Blowfish Gonads Seven diners in Japan became seriously ill with breathing difficulties and limb paralysis after eating grilled blowfish testicles in a restaurant not licensed to serve this particular dish, which is poisonous if not prepared correctly.

A Debt to Spaghetti The shapely Italian film star Sophia Loren denied ever having made the claim frequently attributed to her, namely 'Everything you see I owe to spaghetti.'

2010

Top Nip A record price for whisky was achieved when a 64-year-old Macallan in a 1.5-litre decanter made by René Lalique sold at auction in New York for $460,000 (£280,000). The proceeds went to a clean-water charity.

2011

Corpses Turned into Curry, Allegedly Two brothers were arrested by police in Pakistan and charged with digging up the body of a recently buried 24-year-old woman, and cooking her legs in a curry. Police suggested that the brothers might have been indulging in such practices for a decade, having suffered upset after their mother died and their wives left them. There is no law against cannibalism as such in Pakistan, although it is illegal to desecrate a grave.

Exploding Watermelons in China Farmers in eastern China suffered considerable shock after they applied forchlorfenuron, a growth accelerator, to their watermelon fields. Apparently they sprayed their crops too late in the season, and in wet conditions, with the result that the watermelons exploded 'like landmines'. One farmer, Liu Mingsuo, told China Central Television, the state broadcaster, that one morning he came out and counted 80 burst watermelons; by the afternoon, 20 more had blown apart, sending shrapnel of seeds, skin and flesh in all directions. The overdependence on chemicals in Chinese agriculture has caused widespread alarm, with stories of the heavy metal cadmium in rice, bleach in mushrooms, toxic melamine added to milk, soy sauce laced with arsenic, and pork infused with borax to pass it off as beef.

Beer for Space Tourists Two Australian entrepreneurs, Jaron Mitchell of the 4 Pines Brewing Company and Jason Held of space technology firm Saber Astronautics, announced that they were developing the Vostok 4 Pines Stout, a full-bodied brew designed to be consumed by tourists carried into space either by the Russians or by Richard Branson's proposed Virgin Galactic venture. There are a number of problems to be overcome for a beer to be enjoyed in zero gravity: in such conditions the tongue swells and so reduces the sense of taste; alcohol is absorbed by the body in unpredictable ways; and bubbles and liquid find it difficult to separate, resulting in the uncomfortable phenomenon known as the 'wet burp', when both gas and liquid come out together.

The Horseradish Alarm A group of scientists at the Shiga University of Medical Science in Japan were awarded the

2011 Ig Nobel prize for chemistry in recognition of their work in developing an alarm that can alert deaf people to fire or other emergencies. The alarm works by releasing air-diluted wasabi (Japanese horseradish), which is so pungent that its irritating effect on the nose can wake people up from even the deepest sleep.

The Baby Gaga Breast-Milk Ice Cream Saga The Icecreamists, an ice cream parlour in London's Covent Garden, launched a new line, selling at £14 per portion. This special ice cream, flavoured with Madagascan vanilla pods and lemon zest, and served with a rusk in a cocktail glass, contained a unique ingredient: human breast-milk. Lactating mothers who wished to donate were screened via a blood test, and earned £15 for every 10 ounces extracted using breast pumps. The Icecreamists called their new line 'Baby Gaga', prompting the US singer known as Lady Gaga – who once appeared in a dress made from raw meat – to threaten legal action. The owner of The Icecreamists, Matt O'Connor, came out fighting, telling the press:

> A global superstar has taken umbrage at what she describes as a 'nausea-inducing' product. This from a woman with a penchant for wearing rotting cows' flesh. At least our customers are still alive when they contribute to our 'art'. She claims we have 'ridden

the coattails' of her reputation. As someone who has
. . . recycled on an industrial scale the entire back
catalogue of pop culture to create her look, music
and videos, she might want to reconsider this allega-
tion. How can she possibly claim ownership of the
word 'gaga', which since the dawn of time has been
one of the first discernable phrases to come from a
baby's mouth?

Lady Gaga was not the only one to raise an eyebrow. The
Health Protection Agency and the Food Standards Agency
also voiced their concerns, and as a result the parlour's
stocks of Baby Gaga were removed by officers from West-
minster Council.